DENISE
LEVERTOV
POEMS
1960-1967

Books by Denise Levertov

Poetry

The Double Image

Here and Now

Overland to the Islands

With Eyes at the Back of Our Heads

The Jacob's Ladder

O Taste and See

The Sorrow Dance

Relearning the Alphabet

To Stay Alive

Footprints

The Freeing of the Dust

Life in the Forest

Collected Earlier Poems 1940–1960

Candles in Babylon

Poems 1960–1967

Prose

The Poet in the World

Light Up the Cave

Translations

Guillevic/Selected Poems

DENISE
LEVERTOV
POEMS
1960-1967

A NEW DIRECTIONS BOOK

Grateful acknowledgment is made to the editors and publishers of
magazines and anthologies in which some of the poems in this collec-
tion originally appeared: *Agenda* (London), *Angel Hair, Arts & Sci-
ences, Arts & Society, Beloit Poetry Journal, Big Table, Brown Paper,
Burning Deck, The Catholic Worker, Chelsea, Chicago Choice, The
Chicago Review, Damascus Road, Emerson Review, Fubbalo, Genesis
West, Granta* (England), *Hanging Loose, Harper's, Harper's Bazaar,
The Harvard Advocate, Hip Pocket Poems, The Hudson Review, Jubi-
lee, Love, Magazine, The Massachusetts Review, The Minnesota Re-
view, The Nation, Nation Centennial, The New England Galaxy, The
New Review, The New Statesman, Nomad, North American Review,
Occidental Review, Open Places, Origin, Outburst* (London), *Paris
Review, Peace News* (London), *Poetry, The Quarterly Review, Quar-
terly Review of Literature, Quixote, Rivoli Review, Salon 13* (Guate-
mala), *San Francisco Review, Sisters Today, Some/thing, Sturbridge,
Sum, Synapse, Syracuse 10, Things, University of Tampa Poetry Re-
view, Upriver, Wagner College Literary Magazine, Wild Dog.*

The translations of two poems by Jules Supervielle (" 'Ce bruit de la
mer . . .' " and "Stems") are published by courtesy of Librairie Gal-
limard, Paris.

"The Breathing" was first published in *Poetry in Crystal* by Steuban
Glass. "City Psalm" first appeared as a broadsheet in the Oyez series,
Berkeley, California. "Psalm Concerning the Castle" first appeared as
a broadsheet published by Walter Hamady, Detroit, Michigan.

The quotation from *Tales of the Hasidim: Later Masters*, Copyright
1948 by Schocken Books, Inc., is reprinted by courtesy of the publisher.
The quotation from Louis MacNeice in "Olga Poems," from his *Sol-
stices*, Copyright © 1961 by Louis MacNeice, is reprinted by courtesy
of Oxford University Press, Inc. The quotation from Rainer Maria Rilke
in "Life at War," from *Letters of Rainer Maria Rilke*, Volume Two,
1920–1926, translated by Jane Bannard Greene and M. D. Herter Nor-
ton, Copyright 1947, 1948 by W. W. Norton & Company, Inc., is re-
printed by permission of the publisher. The quotation from Rilke in
"Joy," from *Selected Letters of Rilke*, translated by R. F. C. Hull, is
reprinted by permission of the publisher, Macmillan and Co., Ltd.

Manufactured in the United States of America
First published clothbound and as New Directions Paperbook 549 in
1983
Published simultaneously in Canada by George J. McLeod, Ltd.,
Toronto

Library of Congress Cataloging in Publication Data

Levertov, Denise, 1923–
    Poems, 1960–1967.
    (A New Directions Book)
    Includes index.
    I. Title.
PS3562.E8876A6   1983   811'.54   83–2263
ISBN 0–8112–0858–3
ISBN 0–8112–0859–1 (pbk.)

New Directions Books are published for James Laughlin
by New Directions Publishing Corporation,
80 Eighth Avenue, New York 10011

Contents

THE JACOB's LADDER (1961)

To the Reader

As you read, a white bear leisurely
pees, dyeing the snow
saffron,

and as you read, many gods
lie among lianas: eyes of obsidian
are watching the generations of leaves,

and as you read
the sea is turning its dark pages,
turning
its dark pages.

The Ladder

Rabbi Moshe (of Kobryn) taught:
It is written: "And he dreamed,
and behold a ladder set up on the
earth." That "he" is every man.
Every man must know: I am clay,
I am one of countless shards of clay,
but "the top of it reached to
heaven"—my soul reaches to heav-
en; "and behold the angels of God
ascending and descending on it"—
even the ascent and descent of the
angels depend on my deeds.

Tales of the Hasidim: Later Masters by
Martin Buber.

i

To stand on common ground
here and there gritty with pebbles
yet elsewhere 'fine and mellow—
uncommon fine for ploughing'

there to labor
planting the vegetable words
diversely in their order
that they come to virtue!

To reach those shining pebbles,
that soil where uncommon men
have labored in their virtue
and left a store

of seeds for planting!
To crunch on words
grown in grit or fine
crumbling earth, sweet

to eat and sweet
to be given, to be eaten
in common, by laborer
and hungry wanderer . . .

ii

In time of blossoming,
of red
buds, of red
margins upon
white petals among the
new green, of coppery
leaf-buds still weakly
folded, fuzzed
with silver hairs—

3

when on the grass verges
or elephant-hide rocks, the lunch hour
expands, the girls
laugh at the sun, men
in business suits awkwardly
recline, the petals
float and fall into
crumpled wax-paper, cartons
of hot coffee—

to speak as the sun's
deep tone of May gold speaks
or the spring chill in the rock's shadow,
a piercing minor scale running across the flesh
aslant—or petals
that dream their way
(speaking by being white
by being
curved, green-centered, falling
already while their tree
is half-red with buds) into

human lives! Poems stirred
into paper coffee-cups, eaten
with petals on rye in the
sun—the cold shadows in back,
and the traffic grinding the
borders of spring—entering
human lives forever,
unobserved, a spring element . . .

. . . everything in the world must
excel itself to be itself.

Pasternak

Not 'common speech'
a dead level
but the uncommon speech of paradise,
tongue in which oracles
speak to beggars and pilgrims:

not illusion but what Whitman called
'the path
between reality and the soul,'
a language
excelling itself to be itself,

speech akin to the light
with which at day's end and day's
renewal, mountains
sing to each other across the cold valleys.

i

On the kitchen wall a flash
of shadow:
        swift pilgrimage
of pigeons, a spiral
celebration of air, of sky-deserts.
And on tenement windows
a blaze
      of lustered watermelon:
stain of the sun
westering somewhere back of Hoboken.

ii

The goatherd upstairs! Music
from his sweet flute
roves from summer to summer
in the dusty air of airshafts
and among the flakes
of soot that float
in a daze from chimney
to chimney—notes
remote, cool, speaking of slender
shadows under olive-leaves.   A silence.

iii

Groans, sighs, in profusion,
with coughing, muttering, orchestrate
solitary grief; the crash of glass, a low voice
repeating over and over, 'No.
No. I want my key. No you did not.
No.'—a commonplace.
And in counterpoint, from other windows,
the effort to be merry—ay, maracas!
—sibilant, intricate—the voices wailing pleasure,
        arriving perhaps at joy, late, after sets
have been switched off, and silences
are dark windows?

The Part

In some special way every person
completes the universe. If he does
not play his part, he injures the
pattern of all existence. . . .

Rabbi Judah Loew

Homer da Vinci
with freckles on your nose
don't hang there

by the heels.
Sad everyman, I mean
let go, or jerk
upright.

They say gooseflesh
is the body's shudder when someone
walks over its grave-to-be,

but my hair rises
to see your living life
tamped down.

Blue mysteries
of the veronica florets
entertain
your modest attention:

there, where you live,
live:
start over,
everyman, with
the algae of your dreams.

8

Man gets his daily bread
in sweat, but no one said
in daily death. Don't eat

those nice green dollars your wife
gives you for breakfast.

i

A changing skyline.
A slice of window filled in
by a middle-distance oblong
topped by little
moving figures.
You are speaking
flatly, 'as one drinks a glass of

milk' (for calcium).
          Suddenly the milk
spills, a torrent of black milk hurtles
through the room, bubbling and
seething into the corners.

ii

'But then I was another person!'
The building veiled
in scaffolding. When the builders leave,
tenants will move in, pervading
cubic space with breath and dreams.
Odor of newmade memories
will loiter in the hallways,
noticed by helpless dogs and young children.
That will be other, another
building.

iii

I had meant to say
only, 'The skyline's changing,
the window's allowance of sky is
smaller
          but more
intensely designed, sprinkled
with human gestures.'

10

That's not enough.
Ah, if you've not seen it
it's not enough.
Alright.
It's true.
Nothing

is ever enough. Images
split the truth
in fractions. And milk
of speech is black lava. The sky
is sliced into worthless
glass diamonds.

iv

Again: middle of a night.
Silences lifting
bright eyes that brim with
smiles and painful
stone tears.
                    Will you believe it,
in this very room
cloud-cuckoos unfledged themselves,
shedding feathers and down,
showed themselves small,
monstrous,
paltry in death?
In the dark
when the past lays its hand on your heart,
can't you recall that hour of
death and new daylight?

11

But how irrelevantly
the absurd angel of happiness walks in,
a box of matches in one hand,
in the other a book of dream-jokes.
I wake up laughing, tell you:
'I was writing an
ad for gold—gold cups,
gold porridge-bowls—**Gold,
beautiful, durable**—While I mused
for a third adjective, you were
preparing to leave for
three weeks—**Here's the check. And
perhaps in a week or so
I'll be able to send you a
pound of tomatoes.**' Then
you laugh too, and we clasp
in naked laughter, trembling
with tenderness and relief.
Meanwhile the angel,
dressed for laughs as a plasterer,
puts a match to whatever's
lying in the grate: broken scaffolds,
empty cocoons, the paraphernalia
of unseen change.
Our eyes smart from the smoke but
we laugh and
warm ourselves.

The Rainwalkers

An old man whose black face
shines golden-brown as wet pebbles
under the streetlamp, is walking
two mongrel dogs of dis-
proportionate size, in the rain,
in the relaxed early-evening avenue.

The small sleek one wants to stop,
docile to the imploring soul of the trashbasket,
but the young tall curly one
wants to walk on; the glistening sidewalk
entices him to arcane happenings.

Increasing rain. The old bareheaded man
smiles and grumbles to himself.
The lights change: the avenue's
endless nave echoes notes of
liturgical red. He drifts

between his dogs' desires.
The three of them are enveloped—
turning now to go crosstown—in their
sense of each other, of pleasure,
of weather, of corners,
of leisurely tensions between them
and private silence.

A doll's hair concealing
an eggshell skull delicately
throbbing, within which
maggots in voluptuous unrest
jostle and shrug. Oh, Eileen, my
big doll, your gold hair was
not more sunny than this
human fur, but
your head was
radiant in its emptiness,
a small clean room.

Her warm and rosy mouth
is telling lies—she would
believe them if she could believe:
her pretty eyes
search out corruption. Oh, Eileen,
how kindly your silence was, and
what virtue
shone in the opening and shutting of your
ingenious blindness.

The screendoor whines, clacks
shut.   My thoughts crackle
with seaweed-seething diminishing
flickers of phosphorus.   Gulp
of a frog, plash
of herring leaping;
                    interval;
squawk of a gull disturbed, a splashing;
pause
while silence poises for the breaking
bark of a seal: but silence.
                         Then
only your breathing. I'll
be quiet too. Out
stove, out lamp, let
night cut the question with profound
unanswer, sustained
echo of our unknowing.

While we sleep
mudflats will gleam
in moonwane, and mirror
      earliest wan daybreak
        in pockets and musselshell hillocks, before
a stuttering, through dreams, of
lobsterboats going out, a half-
awakening, a re-

living of ebbing dreams as morning ocean
returns to us, a turning
from light towards more dreams, intelligence of
what pulls at our depths for

design.
I hear

the tide turning. Last
eager wave over-
taken and pulled back
by first wave of the ebb. The pull back
by moon-ache. The great knots
of moon-awake energy
far out.

When the white fog burns off,
the abyss of everlasting light
is revealed. The last cobwebs
of fog in the
black firtrees are flakes
of white ash in the world's hearth.

Cold of the sea is counterpart
to this great fire. Plunging
out of the burning cold of ocean
we enter an ocean of intense
noon. Sacred salt
sparkles on our bodies.

After mist has wrapped us again
in fine wool, may the taste of salt
recall to us the great depths about us.

i

We have been shown
how Basket drank—
and old man Volpe the cobbler
made up what words he didn't know
so that his own son, even
laughed at him: but with respect.

ii

Two flutes! How close
to each other they move
in mazing figures,
never touching, never
breaking the measure,
as gnats dance in
summer haze all afternoon, over
shallow water sprinkled
with mottled blades of willow—
two flutes!

iii

Shlup, shlup, the dog
as it laps up
water
makes intelligent
music, resting
now and then to
take breath in irregular
measure.

18

iv

When I can't
strike one spark from you,
when you don't
look me in the eye,
when your answers
come
        slowly, dragging
their feet, and furrows
change your face,
when the sky is a cellar
with dirty windows,
when furniture
obstructs the body, and bodies
are heavy furniture coated
with dust—time
for a lagging leaden pace,
a short sullen line,
measure
of heavy heart and
cold eye.

v

The quick of the sun that gilds
broken pebbles in sidewalk cement
and the iridescent
spit, that defiles and adorns!
Gold light in blind love does not distinguish
one surface from another, the savor
is the same to its tongue, the fluted
cylinder of a new ashcan a dazzling silver,
the smooth flesh of screaming children a quietness, it is all
a jubilance, the light catches up
the disordered street in its apron,
broken fruitrinds shine in the gutter.

19

vi

Lap up the vowels
of sorrow,
        transparent, cold
water-darkness welling
up from the white sand.
Hone the blade
of a scythe to cut swathes
of light sound in the mind.
Through the hollow globe, a ring
of frayed rusty scrapiron,
is it the sea that shines?
Is it a road at the world's edge?

A Map of the Western Part of the
County of Essex in England

Something forgotten for twenty years: though my fathers
and mothers came from Cordova and Vitepsk and Caernarvon,
and though I am a citizen of the United States and less a
stranger here than anywhere else, perhaps,
I am Essex-born:
Cranbrook Wash called me into its dark tunnel,
the little streams of Valentines heard my resolves,
Roding held my head above water when I thought it was
drowning me; in Hainault only a haze of thin trees
stood between the red doubledecker buses and the boar-hunt,
the spirit of merciful Phillipa glimmered there.
Pergo Park knew me, and Clavering, and Havering-atte-
    Bower,
Stanford Rivers lost me in osier beds, Stapleford Abbots
sent me safe home on the dark road after Simeon-quiet
    evensong,
Wanstead drew me over and over into its basic poetry,
in its serpentine lake I saw bass-viols among the golden dead
    leaves,
through its trees the ghost of a great house. In
Ilford High Road I saw the multitudes passing pale under the
light of flaring sundown, seven kings
in somber starry robes gathered at Seven Kings
the place of law
where my birth and marriage are recorded
and the death of my father. Woodford Wells
where an old house was called The Naked Beauty (a white
statue forlorn in its garden)
saw the meeting and parting of two sisters,
(forgotten? and further away
the hill before Thaxted? where peace befell us? not once
but many times?).
All the Ivans dreaming of their villages
all the Marias dreaming of their walled cities,

21

picking up fragments of New World slowly,
not knowing how to put them together nor how to join
image with image, now I know how it was with you, an old
    map
made long before I was born shows ancient
rights of way where I walked when I was ten burning with
    desire
for the world's great splendors, a child who traced voyages
indelibly all over the atlas, who now in a far country
remembers the first river, the first
field, bricks and lumber dumped in it ready for building,
that new smell, and remembers
the walls of the garden, the first light.

Come into animal presence.
No man is so guileless as
the serpent. The lonely white
rabbit on the roof is a star
twitching its ears at the rain.
The llama intricately
folding its hind legs to be seated
not disdains but mildly
disregards human approval.
What joy when the insouciant
armadillo glances at us and doesn't
quicken his trotting
across the track into the palm brush.

What is this joy? That no animal
falters, but knows what it must do?
That the snake has no blemish,
that the rabbit inspects his strange surroundings
in white star-silence? The llama
rests in dignity, the armadillo
has some intention to pursue in the palm-forest.
Those who were sacred have remained so,
holiness does not dissolve, it is a presence
of bronze, only the sight that saw it
faltered and turned from it.
An old joy returns in holy presence.

In the autumn brilliance
feathers tingle at fingertips.

This tingling brilliance
burns under cover of gray air and

brown lazily
unfalling leaves,

it eats into stillness zestfully
with sound of plucked strings,

steel and brass strings of the zither,
copper and silver wire

played with a gold ring,
a plucking of crinkled afternoons and

evenings of energy, thorns under the pot.
In the autumn brilliance

a drawing apart of curtains
a fall of veils

a flying open of doors, convergence
of magic objects into
feathered hands and crested heads, a prospect
of winter verve, a buildup to abundance.

My black sun, my
Odessa sunflower,
spurs of Tartar gold
ring at your ankles,
you stand taller before me than the ten
towers of Jerusalem.

Your tongue has found
my tongue, peonies
turn their profusion towards
the lamp, it is you that burn there,
the Black Sea sings you awake.

Wake the violoncellos of Lebanon,
rub the bows with cedar resin,
wake the Tundra horsemen
to hunt tigers.
     Your skin
tastes of the salt of Marmora,
the hair of your body casts
its net over me.
     To my closed eyes
appears a curved
horizon where darkness
dazzles in your light. Your arms
hold me from falling.

Among a hundred windows shining
   dully in the vast side
of greater-than-palace number such-and-such
   one burns
these several years, each night
   as if the room within were aflame.
Some fault in the glass
   combines with the precise distance and
my faulty eyes to produce
   this illusion; I know it—
yet still I'm ready to believe perhaps
   some lives
tremble and flare up there, four blocks away
   across the sooty roofs and
the dusk,
   with more intensity than what's lived
behind the other windows,
   and the glowing of those brands of life
shows as seraphic or demonic flames
   visible only to weak and distant eyes.

'. . .Else a great Prince in prison lies'

All that blesses the step of the antelope
all the grace a giraffe lifts to the highest leaves
all steadfastness and pleasant gazing, alien to ennui,
dwell secretly behind man's misery.

Animal face, when the lines
of human fear, knots of a net, become transparent
and your brilliant eyes and velvet muzzle
are revealed, who shall say you are not the face of a man?

In the dense light of wakened flesh
animal man is a prince. As from alabaster
a lucency animates him from heel to forehead.
Then his shadows are deep and not gray.

i   The Weave

The cowdung-colored mud
baked and raised up in random
walls, bears the silken
lips and lashes of erotic
flowers towards a sky of
noble clouds. Accepted
sacramental excrement
supports the ecstatic half-sleep
of butterflies, the slow
opening and closing of brilliant
dusty wings. Bite down
on the bitter stem of your nectared
rose, you know
the dreamy stench of death and fling
magenta shawls delicately
about your brown shoulders laughing.

ii   Corazón

When in bushy hollows between
moonround and moonround of hill, white clouds
loiter arm-in-arm, out of curl,
and sheep in the ravines
vaguely congregate, the heart
of Mexico sits in the rain
not caring to seek shelter,
a blanket of geranium pink drawn up
over his silent mouth.

iii The Rose
(*for B.L.*)

In the green Alameda, near the fountains,
an old man, hands
clasped behind his shabby back
shuffles from rose to rose, stopping
to ponder and inhale, and I
follow him at a distance, discovering
the golden rose, color of bees' fur, odor of honey,
red rose, contralto, roses
of dawn-cloud-color, of snow-in-moonlight,
of colors only roses know,
but no rose
like the rose I saw in your garden.

iv Canticle

Flies, acolytes
of the death-in-life temple
buzz their prayers

and from the altar
of excrement arises
an incense

of orange and purple
petals.   Drink,
campesino,

stain with ferment
the blinding white that clothes
your dark body.

v   Sierra

Golden the high ridge of thy back, bull-mountain,
and coffee-black thy full sides.
The sky decks thy horns with violet,
with cascades of cloud. The brown hills
are thy cows.   Shadows
of zopilotes cross and slowly
cross again
thy flanks, lord of herds.

the only object is
a man, carved
out of himself, so wrought he
fills his given space, makes
traceries sufficient to
others' needs
(here is
social action, for the poet,
anyway, his
politics, his
news)

Charles Olson

Breathe deep of the
freshly gray morning air, mild
spring of the day.
Let the night's dream-planting
bear leaves
and light up the death-mirrors with
shining petals.
Stand fast in thy place:
remember, Caedmon
turning from song was met
in his cow-barn by One who set him
to sing the beginning.
Live
in thy fingertips and in thy
hair's rising; hunger
be thine, food
be thine and what wine
will not shrivel thee.
Breathe deep of
evening, be with the
rivers of tumult, sharpen
thy wits to know power and be
humble.

ii

The task of the poet is to make clear
to *himself,* and thereby to others,
the temporal and eternal questions.

Ibsen

Barbarians
throng the straight roads of
my empire, converging
on black Rome.
There is darkness in me.
Silver sunrays
sternly, in tenuous joy
cut through its folds:
mountains
arise from cloud.
Who was it yelled, cracking
the glass of delight?
Who sent the child
sobbing to bed, and woke it
later to comfort it?
I, I, I, I.
I multitude, I tyrant,
I angel, I you, you
world, battlefield, stirring
with unheard litanies, sounds of piercing
green half-smothered by
strewn bones.

iii

And virtue? Virtue lies in the heroic
response to the creative wonder, the
utmost response.

D. H. Lawrence

Death in the grassblade
a dull
substance, heading blindly
for the bone

32

and bread preserved without
virtue,
sweet grapes sour to the children's children.

We breathe an ill wind,
nevertheless our kind
in mushroom multitudes
jostles for elbow-room
moonwards

an equalization of
hazards
bringing the poet
back to song
as before

to sing of death
as before
and life, while he
has it, energy

being in him a singing,
a beating of gongs, efficacious
to drive away devils,
response to

the wonder that
as before
shows a double face,

to be
what he is
being his virtue

filling his whole space
so no devil
may enter.

i

The day before he died, a burnet moth
come to town perhaps on a load of greens,
took me a half-hour out of my way, or what
I'd thought was my way.   It lay bemused
on the third step down of the subway entrance.
I took it up—it scarcely fluttered. Where
should I take it for safety,
away from hasty feet and rough hands?
We went through the hot streets together,
it lay trustingly in my hand,
awkwardly I shielded it from the dusty
wind, a glitter of brine
hovered about the cement vistas.
At last I found
a scrap of green garden
to hide the stranger, and silently took leave.

Not his soul—
I knew that dwelled always on Russian earth
—yet it was spoken in me
that the dark, narrow-winged, richly
crimson-signed being, an
apparition at the steps to the underworld,
whose need took me upwards again and further than
I had thought to walk, was a word,
an emanation from him, fulfilling
what he had written—'I feel
that we shall be friends.'

Seen through what seem
his eyes (his gift) the gray barn
and the road into the forest,
the snipe's dead young I am burying among
wild-strawberry leaves, all
lifts itself, poises itself to speak:

and the deaf soul
struggles, strains forward, to lip-read what it needs:
and something is said, quickly,
in words of cloud-shadows moving and
the unmoving turn of the road, something
not quite caught, but filtered
through some outpost of dreaming sense
the gist, the drift. I remember
a dream two nights ago: the voice,
'the artist must
create himself or be born again.'

(*after Jules Supervielle*)

That sound, everywhere about us, of the sea—
the tree among its tresses has always heard it,
and the horse dips his black body in the sound
stretching his neck as if towards drinking water,
as if he were longing to leave the dunes and become
a mythic horse in the remotest distance,
joining the flock of foam-sheep—
fleeces made for vision alone—
to be indeed the son of these salt waters
and browse on algae in the deep fields.
But he must learn to wait, wait on the shore,
promising himself **someday** to the waves of the open sea,
putting his hope in certain death, lowering
his head again to the grass.

(after Jules Supervielle)

A poplar tree under the stars,
what can it do.
And the bird in the poplar tree
dreaming, his head
tucked into
far-and-near exile under his wing—
what can either of them
in their confused alliance of
leaves and feathers
do to avert destiny?

Silence and the
ring of forgetting
protect them until the moment when
the sun rises
and memory with it.
Then the bird
breaks with his beak the thread
of dream within him,
and the tree unrolls
the shadow that will guard it
throughout the day.

The head Byzantine or from
Fayyum, the shoulders naked,
a little of the
dark-haired breast visible
above the sheet,

from deep in the dark head
his smile glowing
outward into the
room's severe twilight,

he lies, a dark-shadowed
mellow gold against
the flattened white pillow,
a gentle man—

strength and despair
quiet there in the bed,
the line of his limbs
half-shown, as under stone
or bronze folds.

The stairway is not
a thing of gleaming strands
a radiant evanescence
for angels' feet that only glance in their tread, and need not
touch the stone.

It is of stone.
A rosy stone that takes
a glowing tone of softness
only because behind it the sky is a doubtful, a doubting
night gray.

A stairway of sharp
angles, solidly built.
One sees that the angels must spring
down from one step to the next, giving a little
lift of the wings:

and a man climbing
must scrape his knees, and bring
the grip of his hands into play. The cut stone
consoles his groping feet. Wings brush past him.
The poem ascends.

The Muse
   in her dark habit,
trim-waisted,
    wades into deep water.

The spring where she
   will fill her pitcher to the brim
wells out
   below the lake's surface, among
papyrus, where a stream
   enters the lake and is crossed
by the bridge on which I stand.

She stoops
   to gently dip and deep enough.
Her face resembles
   the face of the young actress who played
Miss Annie Sullivan, she who
   spelled the word 'water' into the palm
of Helen Keller, opening
   the doors of the world.

In the baroque park,
   transformed as I neared the water
   to Valentines, a place of origin,
I stand on a bridge of one span
and see this calm act, this gathering up
   of life, of spring water

and the Muse gliding then
   in her barge without sails, without
oars or motor, across
   the dark lake, and I know

40

no interpretation of these mysteries
    although I know she is the Muse
and that the humble
    tributary of Roding is
one with Alpheus, the god who as a river
    flowed through the salt sea to his love's well

so that my heart leaps
    in wonder.
Cold, fresh, deep, I feel the word 'water'
    spelled in my left palm.

Months after the Muse
had come and gone across the lake of vision,
arose out of childhood the long-familiar
briefly forgotten presaging of her image—

'The Light of Truth'—frontispiece
to 'Parables from Nature,' 1894—a picture
intending another meaning than that which it gave
(for I never read the story until now)

intending to represent Folly
sinking into a black bog, but for me having meant
a mystery, of darkness, of beauty, of serious
dreaming pause and intensity

where not a will-o'-the-wisp but
a star come to earth burned before the
closed all-seeing eyes
of that figure later seen as the Muse.

By which I learn to affirm
Truth's light at strange turns of the mind's road,
wrong turns that lead
over the border into wonder,

mistaken directions, forgotten signs
all bringing the soul's travels to a place
of origin, a well
under the lake where the Muse moves.

i
Osip Mandelstam

With a glass of
boiled water
not yet cold
by a small stove
not giving out
much heat
he was sitting
and saying over
those green words
Laura and laurel
written in Avignon

when out of the somber
winter day entered
Death in green clothing
having traveled
by train and on foot
ten thousand kilometers to
this end,
and moving aside to give him
a place at the fire, the poet
made him welcome, asking
for news of home.

ii
César Vallejo

Darling Death
shouted in his ear,
his ear made to record
the least, the most finespun
of worm-cries and
dragonfly-jubilations,
and with that courtesy he accorded
all clumsy living things
that stumble in broken boots
he bowed and
not flinching from her black breath
gave her his arm and
walked back with her the
way she had come and
turned the corner.

Melody
      moving
            downstream
a string of barges
           just
lit
against blue evening, the fog
giving each light
a halo

moving with
the river but not
adrift, a little
       faster perhaps
   or is it
slower? —a
singing
sung if it is sung
quietly

within the scored
crashing and the
almost inaudible hum impinging
upon the river's
       seawardness

A Letter to William Kinter of Muhlenberg

Zaddik, you showed me
the Stations of the Cross

and I saw
not what the almost abstract

tiles held—world upon world—
but at least

a shadow of what
might be seen there if mind and heart

gave themselves to meditation,
deeper

and deeper into Imagination's
holy forest, as travelers

followed the Zohar's dusty
shimmering roads, talking

with prophets and
hidden angels.

From the bus, Zaddik,
going home to New York,

I saw a new world
for a while—it was

the gold light on a rocky slope,
the road-constructors talking to each other,

bear-brown of winter woods, and later
lights of New Jersey factories and the vast

December moon. I saw
without words within me, saw

as if my eyes
had grown bigger and knew

how to look without
being told what it was they saw.

The clouds as I see them, rising
urgently, roseate in the
mounting of somber power

surging in evening haste over
roofs and hermetic
grim walls—

          Last night
as if death had lit a pale light
in your flesh, your flesh
was cold to my touch, or not cold
but cool, cooling, as if the last traces
of warmth were still fading in you.
My thigh burned in cold fear where
yours touched it.

But I forced to mind my vision of a sky
close and enclosed, unlike the space in which these clouds
     move—
a sky of gray mist it appeared—
and how looking intently at it we saw
its gray was not gray but a milky white
in which radiant traces of opal greens,
fiery blues, gleamed, faded, gleamed again,
and how only then, seeing the color in the gray,
a field sprang into sight, extending
between where we stood and the horizon,

a field of freshest deep spiring grass
starred with dandelions,
green and gold
gold and green alternating in closewoven
chords, madrigal field.

Is death's chill that visited our bed
other than what it seemed, is it
a gray to be watched keenly?

Wiping my glasses and leaning westward,
clearing my mind of the day's mist and leaning
into myself to see
the colors of truth

I watch the clouds as I see them
in pomp advancing, pursuing
the fallen sun.

Something is very gently,
invisibly, silently,
pulling at me—a thread
or net of threads
finer than cobweb and as
elastic. I haven't tried
the strength of it. No barbed hook
pierced and tore me. Was it
not long ago this thread
began to draw me? Or
way back? Was I
born with its knot about my
neck, a bridle? Not fear
but a stirring
of wonder makes me
catch my breath when I feel
the tug of it when I thought
it had loosened itself and gone.

From the Roof

This wild night, gathering the washing as if it were flowers
        animal vines twisting over the line and
        slapping my face lightly, soundless merriment
        in the gesticulations of shirtsleeves,
I recall out of my joy a night of misery

walking in the dark and the wind over broken earth,
        halfmade foundations and unfinished
        drainage trenches and the spaced-out
                circles of glaring light
        marking streets that were to be,
walking with you but so far from you,

and now alone in October's
first decision towards winter, so close to you—
        my arms full of playful rebellious linen, a freighter
        going down-river two blocks away, outward bound,
        the green wolf-eyes of the Harborside Terminal
                glittering on the Jersey shore,
and a train somewhere under ground bringing you towards me
to our new living-place from which we can see

a river and its traffic (the Hudson and the
hidden river, who can say which it is we see, we see
something of both. Or who can say
the crippled broom-vendor yesterday, who passed
just as we needed a new broom, was not
one of the Hidden Ones?)

                    Crates of fruit are unloading
                    across the street on the cobbles,
                    and a brazier flaring
                        to warm the men and burn trash. He wished us
luck when we bought the broom. But not luck
brought us here. By design

clear air and cold wind polish
the river lights, by design
we are to live now in a new place.

The Presence

To the house on the grassy hill
where rams rub their horns against the porch

and your bare feet on the floors of silence
speak in rhymed stanzas to the furniture,

solemn chests of drawers and heavy chairs
blinking in the sun you have let in!

Before I enter the rooms of your solitude
in my living form, trailing my shadow,

I shall have come unseen. Upstairs and down with you
and out across road and rocks to the river

to drink the cold spray. You will believe
a bird flew by the window, a wandering bee

buzzed in the hallway, a wind
rippled the bronze grasses. Or will you

know who it is?

To go by the asters
and breathe
the sweetness that hovers

in August about the tall milkweeds,
without a direct look, seeing
only obliquely what we know

is there—that
sets the heart beating fast!
And through

the field of goldenrod,
the lazily-humming waves of
standing hay, not to look up

at the sea-green bloom on the mountain—
the lips part, a sense
of languor and strength begins

to mount in us. The path leads
to the river pool, cold and
flashing with young trout. The sun

on my whiteness and your
tawny gold. Without looking
I see through my lashes the iridescence

on black curls of sexual hair.

Red tulips
living into their death
flushed with a wild blue

tulips
becoming wings
ears of the wind
jackrabbits rolling their eyes

west wind
shaking the loose pane

some petals fall
with that sound one
listens for

In Sabbath quiet, a street
of closed warehouses and wholesale silence,
Adam Misery, while the cop frisks him

lifts with both hands his lip and
drooping mustache to reveal
horse-teeth for inspection.

                          Nothing
is new to him and he is not afraid.
This is a world. As the artist

extends his world with
one gratuitous flourish—a stroke of white or
a run on the clarinet above the

bass tones of the orchestra—so he
ornaments his with
fresh contempt.

The Fountain

Don't say, don't say there is no water
to solace the dryness at our hearts.
I have seen

the fountain springing out of the rock wall
and you drinking there. And I too
before your eyes

found footholds and climbed
to drink the cool water.

The woman of that place, shading her eyes,
frowned as she watched—but not because
she grudged the water,

only because she was waiting
to see we drank our fill and were
refreshed.

Don't say, don't say there is no water.
That fountain is there among its scalloped
green and gray stones,

it is still there and always there
with its quiet song and strange power
to spring in us,
up and out through the rock.

From love one takes
petal to **rock** and **blesséd**
away towards
descend,

one took thought
for frail tint and spectral
glisten, trusted
from way back that stillness,

one knew
that heart of fire, rose
at the core of gold glow,
could go down undiminished,

for love and
or if in fear knowing
the risk, knowing
what one is touching, one does it,

each part
of speech a spark
awaiting redemption, each
a virtue, a power

in abeyance unless we
give it care
our need designs in us. Then
all we have led away returns to us.

i

The authentic! Shadows of it
sweep past in dreams, one could say imprecisely,
evoking the almost-silent
ripping apart of giant
sheets of cellophane. No.
It thrusts up close. Exactly in dreams
it has you off-guard, you
recognize it before you have time.
For a second before waking
the alarm bell is a red conical hat, it
takes form.

ii

The authentic! I said
rising from the toilet seat.
The radiator in rhythmic knockings
spoke of the rising steam.
The authentic, I said
breaking the handle of my hairbrush as I
brushed my hair in
rhythmic strokes: That's it,
that's joy, it's always
a recognition, the known
appearing fully itself, and
more itself than one knew.

iii

The new day rises
as heat rises,

knocking in the pipes
with rhythms it seizes for its own
to speak of its invention—
the real, the new-laid
egg whose speckled shell
the poet fondles and must break
if he will be nourished.

iv

A shadow painted where
yes, a shadow must fall.
The cow's breath
not forgotten in the mist, in the
words. Yes,
verisimilitude draws up
heat in us, zest
to follow through,
follow through,
follow
transformations of day
in its turning, in its becoming.

v

Stir the holy grains, set
the bowls on the table and
call the child to eat.

While we eat we think,
as we think an undercurrent
of dream runs through us
faster than thought
towards recognition.

Call the child to eat,
send him off, his mouth
tasting of toothpaste, to go down
into the ground, into a roaring train
and to school.

His cheeks are pink
his black eyes hold his dreams, he has left
forgetting his glasses.

Follow down the stairs at a clatter
to give them to him and save
his clear sight.

Cold air
comes in at the street door.

vi

The authentic! It rolls
just out of reach, beyond
running feet and
stretching fingers, down
the green slope and into
the black waves of the sea.
Speak to me, little horse, beloved,
tell me
how to follow the iron ball,
how to follow through to the country
beneath the waves
to the place where I must kill you and you step out
of your bones and flystrewn meat
tall, smiling, renewed,
formed in your own likeness

Marvelous Truth, confront us
at every turn,
in every guise, iron ball,
egg, dark horse, shadow,
cloud
of breath on the air,

dwell
in our crowded hearts
our steaming bathrooms, kitchens full of
things to be done, the
ordinary streets.

Thrust close your smile
that we know you, terrible joy.

During the Eichmann Trial

i   When We Look Up

> When we look up
> each from his being
> *Robert Duncan*

He had not looked,
pitiful man whom none

pity, whom all
must pity if they look

into their own face (given
only by glass, steel, water

barely known) all
who look up

to see—how many
faces?   How many

seen in a lifetime? (Not those
that flash by, but those

into which the gaze wanders
and is lost

and returns to tell
Here is a mystery,

a person, an
other, an I?

Count them.
Who are five million?)

'I was used from the nursery
to obedience

all my life . . .
Corpselike

obedience.' Yellow
calmed him later—

'a charming picture'
yellow of autumn leaves in

Wienerwald, a little
railroad station
nineteen-o-eight, Lemburg,

yellow sun
on the stepmother's teatable

Franz Joseph's beard
blessing his little ones.

It was the yellow
of the stars too,

stars that marked
those in whose faces

you had not
looked. 'They were cast out

as if they were
some animals, some beasts.'

'And what would disobedience
have brought me? And

whom would it have served?'
'I did not let my thoughts

dwell on this—I had
seen it and that was

enough.' (The words
'slur into a harsh babble')

'A spring of blood
gushed from the earth.'
Miracle

unsung. I see
a spring of blood gush from the earth—

Earth cannot swallow
so much at once

a fountain
rushes towards the sky

unrecognized
a sign—.

Pity this man who saw it
whose obedience continued—

he, you, I, which shall I say?
He stands

isolate in a bulletproof
witness-stand of glass,

a cage, where we may view
ourselves, an apparition

telling us something he
does not know: we are members

one of another.

ii The Peachtree

The Danube orchards
are full of fruit
but in the city one tree
haunts a boy's dreams

a tree in a villa garden
the Devil's garden
a peach tree

and of its fruit one peach
calls to him

he sees it yellow and ripe
the vivid blood
bright in its round cheek

Next day he knows
he cannot withstand desire
it is no common fruit

it holds some secret
it speaks to the yellow star within him

he scales the wall
enters the garden of death
takes the peach
and death pounces

mister death who rushes out
from his villa
mister death who loves yellow

who wanted that yellow peach
for himself
mister death who signs papers
then eats

66

telegraphs simply: **Shoot them**
then eats
mister death who orders
more transports
then eats

he would have enjoyed
the sweetest of all the peaches on his tree
with sour-cream
with brandy

Son of David
's blood, vivid red
and trampled juice
yellow and sweet
flow together beneath the tree

there is more blood than
sweet juice
always more blood—mister
death goes indoors
exhausted

Note: This poem is based on the earliest mention, during the trial, of
this incident. In a later statement it was said that the fruit was cherries,
that the boy was already in the garden, doing forced labor, when he
was accused of taking the fruit, and that Eichmann killed him in a tool
shed, not beneath the tree. The poem therefore is not to be taken as a
report of what happened but of what I envisioned.

From blacked-out streets
   (wide avenues swept by curfew,
   alleyways, veins
   of dark within dark)

from houses whose walls
   had for a long time known
the tense stretch of skin over bone
as their brick or stone listened—

      The scream!
The awaited scream rises,
the shattering
of glass and the cracking
of bone

a polar tumult as when
black ice booms, knives
of ice and glass
splitting and splintering the silence into
innumerable screaming needles of
yes, now it is upon us, the jackboots
are running in spurts of
sudden blood-light through the
broken temples

the veils
are rent in twain

terror has a white sound
every scream
of fear is a white needle freezing the eyes
the floodlights of their trucks throw
jets of white, their shouts
cleave the wholeness of darkness into
sectors of transparent white-clouded pantomime
where all that was awaited
is happening, it is Crystal Night

it is Crystal Night
these spikes which are not
pitched in the range of common hearing
whistle through time

smashing the windows of sleep and dream
smashing the windows of history
a whiteness scattering
in hailstones
each a mirror
for man's eyes.

A blind man. I can stare at him
ashamed, shameless. Or does he know it?
No, he is in a great solitude.

O, strange joy,
to gaze my fill at a stranger's face.
No, my thirst is greater than before.

In his world he is speaking
almost aloud. His lips move.
Anxiety plays about them. And now joy

of some sort trembles into a smile.
A breeze I can't feel
crosses that face as if it crossed water.

The train moves uptown, pulls in and
pulls out of the local stops. Within its loud
jarring movement a quiet,

the quiet of people not speaking,
some of them eyeing the blind man,
only a moment though, not thirsty like me,

and within that quiet his
different quiet, not quiet at all, a tumult
of images, but what are his images,

he is blind? He doesn't care
that he looks strange, showing
his thoughts on his face like designs of light

flickering on water, for he doesn't know
what **look** is.
I see he has never seen.

And now he rises, he stands at the door ready,
knowing his station is next. Was he counting?
No, that was not his need.

When he gets out I get out.
'Can I help you towards the exit?'
'Oh, alright.' An indifference.

But instantly, even as he speaks,
even as I hear indifference, his hand
goes out, waiting for me to take it,

and now we hold hands like children.
His hand is warm and not sweaty,
the grip firm, it feels good.

And when we have passed through the turnstile,
he going first, his hand at once
waits for mine again.

'Here are the steps. And here we turn
to the right. More stairs now.' We go
up into sunlight. He feels that,

the soft air. 'A nice day,
isn't it?' says the blind man. Solitude
walks with me, walks

71

beside me, he is not with me, he continues
his thoughts alone. But his hand and mine
know one another,

it's as if my hand were gone forth
on its own journey. I see him
across the street, the blind man,

and now he says he can find his way. He knows
where he is going, it is nowhere, it is filled
with presences. He says, **I am.**

O TASTE AND SEE (1964)

The moon is a sow
and grunts in my throat
Her great shining shines through me
so the mud of my hollow gleams
and breaks in silver bubbles

She is a sow
and I a pig and a poet

When she opens her white
lips to devour me I bite back
and laughter rocks the moon

In the black of desire
we rock and grunt, grunt and
shine

Elves are no smaller
than men, and walk
as men do, in this world,
but with more grace than most,
and are not immortal.

Their beauty sets them aside
from other men and from women
unless a woman has that cold fire in her
called poet: with that

she may see them and by its light
they know her and are not afraid
and silver tongues of love
flicker between them.

The ache of marriage:

thigh and tongue, beloved,
are heavy with it,
it throbs in the teeth

We look for communion
and are turned away, beloved,
each and each

It is leviathan and we
in its belly
looking for joy, some joy
not to be known outside it

two by two in the ark of
the ache of it.

Your beauty, which I lost sight of once
for a long time, is long,
not symmetrical, and wears
the earth colors that make me see it.

A long beauty, what is that?
A song
that can be sung over and over,
long notes or long bones.

Love is a landscape the long mountains
define but don't
shut off from the
unseeable distance.

In fall, in fall,
your trees stretch
their long arms in sleeves
of earth-red and

sky-yellow. I take
long walks among them. The grapes
that need frost to ripen them

are amber and grow deep in the
hedge, half-concealed,
the way your beauty grows in long tendrils
half in darkness.

Cross-country, out of sea fog
comes a letter in dream: a Bard
claims from me 'on whose land they grow,'
seeds of the forget-me-not.

'I ask you
to gather them for me,' says
the Spirit of Poetry.
                    The varied blue
in small compass. In multitude
a cloud of blue, a river
beside the brown river.

Not flowers but
their seeds, I am to send him.
And he bids me
remember my nature, speaking of it
as of a power.
And gather
the flowers, and the flowers
of 'labor' (pink in the dream,
a bright centaury with more petals.
Or the form changes to a sea-pink.)

*Ripple of blue in which are
distinct blues. Bold
centaur-seahorse-salt-carnation
flower of work and transition.*
Out of sea fog, from a hermitage,
at break of day.

Shall I find them, then—
here on my own land, recalled
to my nature?
                    O, great Spirit!

An absolute
patience.
Trees stand
up to their knees in
fog. The fog
slowly flows
uphill.
        White
cobwebs, the grass
leaning where deer
have looked for apples.
The woods
from brook to where
the top of the hill looks
over the fog, send up
not one bird.
So absolute, it is
no other than
happiness itself, a breathing
too quiet to hear.

This is the year the old ones,
the old great ones
leave us alone on the road.

The road leads to the sea.
We have the words in our pockets,
obscure directions. The old ones

have taken away the light of their presence,
we see it moving away over a hill
off to one side.

They are not dying,
they are withdrawn
into a painful privacy

learning to live without words.
E.P. "It looks like dying"—Williams: "I can't
describe to you what has been

happening to me"—
H.D. "unable to speak."
The darkness

twists itself in the wind, the stars
are small, the horizon
ringed with confused urban light-haze.

They have told us
the road leads to the sea,
and given

the language into our hands.
We hear
our footsteps each time a truck

has dazzled past us and gone
leaving us new silence.
One can't reach

the sea on this endless
road to the sea unless
one turns aside at the end, it seems,

follows
the owl that silently glides above it
aslant, back and forth,

and away into deep woods.

But for us the road
unfurls itself, we count the
words in our pockets, we wonder

how it will be without them, we don't
stop walking, we know
there is far to go, sometimes

we think the night wind carries
a smell of the sea. . .

Paradise, an
endless movie. You
walk in, sit down in the dark, it
draws you into itself.

Slowly
an old man crosses
the field of vision, his passions
gathering to the brim of his soul.
And grasses
bow and straighten,

the pulse of wind irregular,
gleam of twilight.

Anything, the attention
never wavers. A woman, say,
who is sleeping or laughing or making
coffee.
A marriage.

Stir of time, the sequence
returning upon itself, branching
a new way. To suffer, pains, hope.
The attention
lives in it as a poem lives or a song
going under the skin of memory.

Or, to believe it's there
within you
though the key's missing

makes it enough? As if
golden pollen were falling

onto your hair from dark trees.

On white linen the silk
of gray shadows
threefold, over-
lapping, a
tau cross.
Glass jug and
tumblers rise from
that which they
cast.

And luminous
in each
overcast of
cylindrical shade,
image
of water, a brightness
not gold, not silver,
rippling
as if with laughter.

In today's mail a poem
quotes from Ecclesiastes:
Whatsoever thy hand
findeth to do, do it with thy might:
for there is no work,
nor device,
nor knowledge,
nor wisdom,
in the grave, whither thou goest.
A letter with it
discloses, in its words and between them,
a life opening, fearful, fearless,
thousand-eyed, a field
of sparks that move swiftly
in darkness, to and from
a center. He is beginning
to live.
The threat
of world's end is the old threat.
'Prepare
for the world to come as thou shouldest
die tomorrow' says
the Book of Delight,
and:
'Prepare for this world as thou
shouldst live forever.'

In the gold mouth of a flower
the black smell of spring earth.
No more skulls on our desks

but the pervasive
testing of death—as if we had need
of new ways of dying? No,

we have no need
of new ways of dying.
Death in us goes on

testing the wild
chance of living
as Adam chanced it.

Golden-mouth, the tilted smile
of the moon westering
is at the black window,

Calavera of Spring.
Do you mistake me?
I am speaking of living,

of moving from one moment into
the next, and into the
one after, breathing

death in the spring air, knowing
air also means
music to sing to.

Turtle Goddess
she of the hard shell
soft underneath
awaits enormously
in a dark grotto
the young Heroes—

Then the corridor
of booths—in each
Life enshrined in
veils of light, scenes
of bliss or
dark action.
Honey and fog, the nose
confused.

And at the corridor's end
two steps
down into Nothing—

The film is over
we're out in the street—

The film-maker's wife grieves and tells him
good-by for ever, you were wrong,
wrong to have shown the Turtle Mother.
The darkness
should not be revealed.
Farewell.

Maker of visions
he walks with me
to the gate of Home and leaves me.
I enter.

Mother is gone,
only Things remain.

So be it.

The pastor
of grief and dreams

guides his flock towards
the next field

with all his care.
He has heard

the bell tolling
but the sheep

are hungry and need
the grass, today and

every day. Beautiful
his patience, his long

shadow, the rippling
sound of the flock moving

along the valley.

Two girls discover
the secret of life
in a sudden line of
poetry.

I who don't know the
secret wrote
the line. They
told me

(through a third person)
they had found it
but not what it was
not even

what line it was. No doubt
by now, more than a week
later, they have forgotten
the secret,

the line, the name of
the poem. I love them
for finding what
I can't find,

and for loving me
for the line I wrote,
and for forgetting it
so that

a thousand times, till death
finds them, they may
discover it again, in other
lines

in other
happenings. And for
wanting to know it,
for

assuming there is
such a secret, yes,
for that
most of all.

The cave downstairs,
jet, obsidian, ember
of bloodstone, glisten
of mineral green.
And what
hangs out there
asleep.

If a serpent were singing,
what silence.
Sleeping, sleeping,
it is the
thunder of the serpent
drumroll of
the mounting smell of

gas.
Unable to wake, to
blurt out the unworded
warning. . .

Augh!

Transformed.
A silence
of waking at night into speech.

He says the waves in the ship's wake
are like stones rolling away.
I don't see it that way.
But I see the mountain turning,
turning away its face as the ship
takes us away.

I have heard it said,
and by a wise man,
that you are not one who comes and goes

but having chosen
you remain in your human house,
and walk

in its garden for air and the delights
of weather and seasons.

Who builds
a good fire in his hearth
shall find you at it
with shining eyes and a ready tongue.

Who shares
even water and dry bread with you
will not eat without joy

and wife or husband
who does not lock the door of the marriage
against you, finds you

not as unwelcome third in the room, but as
the light of the moon on flesh and hair.

He told me, that wise man,
that when it seemed the house was
empty of you,

the fire crackling for no one,
the bread hard to swallow in solitude,
the gardens a tedious maze,

you were not gone away
but hiding yourself in secret rooms.
The house is no cottage, it seems,

it has stairways, corridors, cellars,
a tower perhaps,
unknown to the host.

The host, the housekeeper, it is
who fails you. He had forgotten
to make room for you at the hearth
or set a place for you at the table
or leave the doors unlocked for you.

Noticing you are not there
(when did he last see you?)
he cries out you are faithless,

have failed him,
writes you stormy letters demanding you return
it is intolerable

to maintain this great barracks without your presence,
it is too big, it is too small, the walls
menace him, the fire smokes

and gives off no heat. But to what address
can he mail the letters?
                                And all the while

you are indwelling,
a gold ring lost in the house.
A gold ring lost in the house.
You are in the house!

Then what to do to find the room where you are?
Deep cave of obsidian glowing with red, with green,
with black light,
high room in the lost tower where you sit spinning,

crack in the floor where the gold ring
waits to be found?

                    No more rage but a calm face,
trim the fire, lay the table, find some
flowers for it: is that the way?
Be ready with quick sight to catch
a gleam between the floorboards,

there, where he had looked
a thousand times and seen nothing?
                            Light of the house,

the wise man spoke
words of comfort. You are near,
perhaps you are sleeping and don't hear.

Not even a wise man
can say, do thus and thus, that presence
will be restored.
                    Perhaps

a becoming aware a door is swinging, as if
someone had passed through the room a moment ago—perhaps
looking down, the sight
of the ring back on its finger?

While snow fell carelessly
floating indifferent in eddies of
rooftop air, circling the black
chimney cowls,

a spring night entered
my mind through the tight-closed window,
wearing

a loose Russian shirt of
light silk.
       For this, then,
that slanting
line was left, that crack, the pane
never replaced.

Old Day the gardener seemed
Death himself, or Time, scythe in hand

by the sundial and freshly-dug
grave in my book of parables.

The mignonette, the dusty miller and silvery
rocks in the garden next door

thrived in his care (the rocks
not hidden by weeds but clear-

cut between tufts
of fern and saxifrage). Now

by our peartree with pruning-hook,
now digging the Burnes's neat, weedless

rosebeds, or as he peered
at a bird in Mrs. Peach's laburnum,

his tall stooped person appeared, and gray
curls. He worked

slow and in silence, and knew perhaps
every garden around the block, gardens

we never saw, each one,
bounded by walls of old brick,

a square plot that was
world to itself.

When I was grown
and gone from home he remembered me

in the time of my growing, and sent,
year by year, salutations,

until there was no one there, in
changed times, to send them by. Old Day,

old Death, dusty
gardener, are you

alive yet, do I live on
yet, in your gray

considering eye?

In June the bush we call
alder was heavy, listless,
its leaves studded with galls,

growing wherever we didn't
want it. We cut it
savagely, hunted it from the pasture, chopped it

away from the edge of the wood.
In July, still everywhere, it appeared
wearing green berries.

Anyway it must go. It takes
the light and air and the good of the earth
from flowers and young trees.

But now in August
its berries are red. Do the birds
eat them?   Swinging

clusters of red, the hedges are full of them,
red-currant red, a graceful
ornament or a merry smile.

Quick! there's that
low brief **whirr** to tell

Rubythroat is at the
tigerlilies—

only a passionate baby
sucking breastmilk's so

intent. **Look**
sharply after your thoughts said
Emerson, a good
dreamer.

Worlds may lie
between you
and the bird's return. Hummingbird

stays for a fractional sharp
sweetness, and's gone, can't take

more than that.
The remaining
tigerblossoms have rolled their petals
all the way back,

the stamens protrude entire,
there are no more buds.

To come to the river
the brook
hurtles through rainy
woods, over-
topping rocks that
before the rain were
islands.

Its clearness
is gone, and
the song.
It is a rich brown, a load
of churned earth
goes with it.

The sound now
is a direct, intense
sound of
direction.

A deep wooden note
when the wind blows,
the west wind.
The rock maple is it,
close to the house?
Or a beam, voice
of the house itself?
A groan, but not
gloomy, rather
an escaped note of
almost unbearable
satisfaction, a great
bough or beam
unaware it had
spoken.

i

The All-Day Bird, the artist,
whitethroated sparrow,
striving
in hope and
good faith to make his notes
ever more precise, closer
to what he knows.

ii

There is the proposition
and the development.
The way
one grows from the other.
The All-Day Bird
ponders.

iii

May the first note
be round enough
and those that follow
fine, fine as
sweetgrass,
            prays
the All-Day Bird.

iv

Fine
as the tail of a lizard,
as a leaf of
chives—
the *shadow of a difference*
falling between
note and note,
a *hair's breadth*
defining them.

v

The dew is on the vineleaves.
My tree
is lit with the
break of day.

vi

Sun
light.
    Light
light light light.

A man growing old is going
down the dark stairs.
He has been speaking of the Soul
tattooed with the Law.
Of dreams
burnt in the bone.

He looks up
to the friends who lean
out of light and wine
over the well of stairs.
They ask his pardon
for the dark they can't help.

Starladen Babylon
buzzes in his blood, an ancient
pulse. The rivers
run out of Eden.
Before Adam
Adam blazes.

'It's alright,' answers
the man going down,
'it's alright—there are many
avenues, many corridors of the soul
that are dark also.
Shalom.'

The eastern sky at sunset taking
the glow of the west:
         the west a clear stillness.

The east flinging
nets of cloud
to hold the rose light a moment longer:
         the western hill dark to blackness.

The ants
on their acropolis
prepare for the night.

. . . .

The vine among the rocks
heavy with grapes

the shadows of September
among the gold glint of the grass

among shining
willow leaves the small birds moving

silent in the presence of a new season.

. . . .

In the last sunlight
human figures dark on the hill
outlined—

a fur of gold
about their shoulders and heads,
a blur defining them.

. . . .

Down by the fallen fruit in the old orchard
the air grows cold. The hill
hides the sun.

A sense of the present
rises out of earth and grass,
enters the feet, ascends

into the genitals, constricting
the breast, lightening
the head—a wisdom,

a shiver, a delight
that what is passing

is here, as if
a snake went by, green in the
gray leaves.

In hollows of the land
in faults and valleys
          the white fog
bruised
     by blue shadows
a mirage of lakes

and in the human
faults and depths
           silences
floating
     between night and daybreak
illusion and substance.

But is illusion
so repeated, known
         each dawn,
silence
     suspended in the
mind's shadow

always, not substance
of a sort?
     the white
bruised
     ground-mist the mirage
of a true lake.

A woman had been picking flowers in the half-wild garden of an old farmhouse. Before going indoors to put the flowers in water and begin making supper, she walked around to the back of the house and up the pasture a little way to look across the valley at the hills. The pasture sloped steeply up to a line of trees and a stone wall half-concealed with vines and bushes, then beyond that up again to where the woods began.

The woman waded through the uncut grass and the milkweeds—not yet in flower—to a corner near the stone wall. Beyond this point—the highest point near the house from which to look to the eastern horizon—the ground dropped toward the curving road in a tangle of bracken, alder, young birches. Away across the valley, the unseen meadows of the intervale, she could see the nearest dark green hills, strong presences; and here and there, where these dipped, or sometimes higher than their highest ridges, another rank, green too but lightly dusted with distance. The woman was glad to be able to see them. She felt herself nourished by the sense of distance, by the stillness and mass of the hills. They were called mountains, locally; and they were almost mountains. They had the dignity of mountains. She couldn't quite bring herself to call them mountains, herself, having known higher ones—towering, unforested, sharp-peaked and snowy. But these old hills, rounded, softened by their woods, gave her joy in any case. A few white clouds followed each other across the sky, and their shadows moved darkly over the hills revealing contours the full sun did not show. The afternoon hummed with insects. The stems of the irises she had picked near the driveway felt cool in her hand. Not far away she could hear the voices of her son and her husband. They were cutting brush in the upper part of the pasture.

A view of the hills and a feeling of openness around the house were as important to her husband as to herself. This was their first whole summer here—they had bought the old farm, its fields mostly gone back to woodland, two years ago— and he had spent most of his free time, in these first weeks of it, cutting back the alder bushes that threatened to take over the pasture. The boy liked to help him. Each day, too, they pulled up innumerable milkweeds and dug out dock and burdock from around the edges of the dooryard.

It was still hot in the fields though the shadows were lengthening. Soon they would be coming in, sweaty and hungry. She turned to go, sighing deeply with pleasure. But her last look at the horizon as she turned revealed a flaw she had not realized before: in a great dip of the ridge, to the northeast, some still more distant, and higher, hills—mountains—would have been visible from this lookout, had not a tall and full poplar tree blocked the view. She could glimpse the pale blue of them on either side of its rippling leaves.

At supper the man was speaking of the alders he had cut and meant to cut. The alders were not beautiful and grew with a weedlike insistence. If one did not keep after them they would smother everything. She agreed. There was a coarseness to the leaf, a formlessness about the whole plant, one could not love. The boy—who when this clearing of brush began a week or so before had opposed it, almost with tears, frightened of changing what was already good—was full of pride and enthusiasm for the work done that day. So far they had worked only with machetes and a pair of bush-cutters or with their bare hands, but soon they would get a man with a power-saw to come and fell some of the trees that were crowding each other out. And there were others they could fell with an axe—not wholesale but with judgment—to reveal the form of the land and give back some of the space years of neglect had stolen, the man added.

"I know one tree that needs cutting," the woman said, speaking suddenly as if she had been holding it back and the words had now pushed their way out of her by themselves.

114

"Where's that?" her husband asked, looking up from his plate, his fork poised.

"Well—it's up there beyond that corner . . . I'll show you. There are some far-away mountains one could see from there, but it gets in the way."

The meal continued, they talked of other things, the woman went back and forth between the kitchen and the dining table with dirty plates and dessert and coffee. She was smoking a cigarette and sitting idle while the boy cleared the table when her husband said to her, "Come out a moment and show me which tree you mean."

She looked up at him as if she had not heard what he said.

"Let's go out and look at that tree," he said.

Only a few days before they had gone to picnic near an abandoned hill farm that had seemed, the summer before, very beautiful in its dreaming solitude, as if at rest after a life of achievement; but they found a year's growth of the eager woods had begun to close it in, block the horizon. She had been melancholy there; the blackflies were biting, the grass around the old house had been long and rank, brambles had almost hidden the wellhead and the rhubarb patch. They had eaten quickly, feeling bad tempered, and left almost at once. It had made him very eager to preserve the feeling of lightness and calm there was about their own place.

The woman looked at him and stood up, brushing away a slight unease she felt.

"Come on out with us," the man said to the boy, who was scraping the plates over a box of garbage before stacking them. "We can still do a bit more before the light goes."

The man put an arm around the woman's shoulder as they came out of the kitchen door and began stepping unevenly up the diagonal slope toward the stone wall and the line of trees. In his free hand he carried an axe. The boy followed them whistling. He had the two machetes with him. When they came to the lookout corner she stopped.

115

"Which tree did you mean?" the man asked.

"It's that popple—look—that tall one."

"Oh, yes—you're right. Yes, that would make a big difference. Funny we didn't notice it before."

The tree was one of the common field poplars people called popples, which grew almost as thick as alders in the neglected lands of a once-prosperous farming country. But where the alders were dull leaved and somehow shapeless, the little poplars were always graceful, and she loved their tremulous ways, the gray green of bark and leaves. In the upper pasture they advanced from the woods into the open in little lines as if hand in hand. They must not be allowed to take over, but a few should remain, to catch the light and the breezes. This one, however, grew not in the open grass but out of what was already a thicket of smaller popple, alder and bramble. The white blossom of the blackberry bushes glimmered in the fading light. The tree that was to be felled grew on the downslope but was tall enough to far overtop the line of the northeast horizon, and full enough to block off almost all of that swooping valley among the nearer hills beyond which lay the far-away mountains she longed to see.

The man and the boy after a moment's pause had gone on down the slope and were hidden now behind the bushes. The woman stood looking at the tree. The sun was just gone down, in back of her, but the eastern sky, which had clouded over while they were indoors, was not yet dark. Dove grays were flushed with wild-flower hues of mauve and pink, the white edges of high cumulus were veiled in transparent gold. The tree's gray green was still more green than gray. It stood at just such a distance from her that she could hear the voices of her husband and son, who were struggling now with the tangle of brush that surrounded it, but could not distinguish their words unless they shouted. As she looked, a rift in the clouds gave to the poplar's topmost branches a last gleam of sunlight which began almost immediately to fade. A thrill

116

of wind ran through the tree, and its leaves even in the dulled light flickered like sequins. No other tree picked up the wind until after the poplar had rippled with it, but as the poplar grew almost still again all the lower trees began to stir. The rustling passed from tree to tree until if she closed her eyes she could think herself on a pebble beach. It slowly hushed, a wave powerfully sucking small pebbles and shells with it in its retreat, and no wave succeeded it.

Now the man and the boy had evidently come right up to the trunk of the tree. By the sound of their voices she knew they were arguing about what angle to begin chopping from. A wood thrush was singing somewhere beyond them. The woman began to feel cold, and pulled down the rolled sleeves of her sweater, nervously. She was ill at ease. There was every reason for the tree to come down; she knew those mountains were more truly mountains than the nearer ones that could already be seen; they were more truly mountains not only because of their height and their defined forms but because of their distance. She knew that on days when a sense of triviality or of nagging anxiety beset her, the sight of them, so far removed from her, would give her courage. But the tree stood out from among the blur of many trees, differentiated, poised in air, a presence, and her word had condemned it. She had spoken so quickly; it had been as if she had heard herself speaking words she had not first spoken in herself. And at once these actions began. Could she not have retracted, not shown the tree—or put off showing it for tonight at least? Or even now she could go down the slope and beg off—he would disagree but he would respect her feeling; and the boy would laugh at her or be indignant at her caprice, but within himself he would understand!

The disputing voices were silent but something was delaying the use of the axe. Swishing and hacking sounds, the rustle of pushed-aside leaves, told her they were still cutting away the bushes near the trunk. "So the axe can swing free," she thought. She stood as if unable to move, crossing her arms tightly as the evening grew colder. Her husband was

117

full of a new liveliness these days. He moved from his desk to the fields and back again with a new lightness, as if such transitions were easy or as if there were no question of transition, as if the use of the mind and the use of the body were all one rhythm. She knew that was good, that was the way life should be lived. Could she—with her persistent sense of the precariousness of happiness, the knife-edge balance of his confidence, of all sureness—could she run to him now with a plea to stop what she had begun? To stop, when it was as much in his concern for her needs as for any need of his own to see those particular mountains, that he was felling this tree?

And while she stood came the first blow of the axe. Thwock. The leaves of a poplar are never completely still; but as yet there was no increase in their rippling. Thwock. The tree seemed to her to grow taller, to stretch itself, to smile in the sequin freedom of its flickering leaves. Thwock. With the third blow the whole tree moved—the trunk with a convulsive jerk and the leaves and branches shuddering deeply.

There was a pause. A murmur of voices, the tree seeming to hold its breath. The woman brushed away insects that were biting her bare legs and buzzing around her ears. Another phrase came from the thrush, from further away. The colors were gone from the sky now; the light that remained was toneless. All the varied greens of the woods had become a single dull green. Should she go down close to the tree and see the axe breaking into it? She had never been close to it, never touched its trunk. Should she go back to the house, heat the water and wash the dishes? The tree was as good as felled now, it was too late to stop it. How fearful when possibility becomes irremediable fact! But she remained where she stood, sullenly enduring the biting of the flies and mosquitoes that had gathered around her, not even trying again to wave them away with a piece of bracken.

The blows of the axe resumed. At each blow the tree shook a little, but after that first great jerk and shudder it was as if it only patiently awaited its fall. But how long it took! How could it take so long to hack through quite a slender stem? She heard her husband give a short roar through clenched teeth. Then it seemed the boy was taking a turn at the axe. The blows came hastily one after another, but not so loud. And now the man had the axe again—slowly, heavily, thwock. Thwock.

"Now!" came the boy's voice high and loud, a yell. Very slowly at first the tree began to lean away backwards, then with gathering momentum it was falling, had fallen. The crash was no louder than the sound a man or a large animal might make, shouldering roughly through the thicket. The man let out a low shout of triumph.

The woman began to run clumsily downhill toward them but caught her foot in something, stumbled, and stopped, her heart beating fast and a feeling of loneliness and confusion overwhelming her.

"Did you see it fall?" the boy cried, coming up to her, breathlessly.

"It was a lot tougher than I expected," her husband said, drawing near, smiling warmly and pushing the sweat off his forehead. He turned to see what had been revealed.

"Wow! That was worth doing. Just look at that!"

They gazed through and beyond the space the poplar had occupied. There to the northeast, in the scooped-out hollow of the pass, was an area of unclouded sky still pale with the last of daylight, and against it the far mountains were ranged, a wistful blue, remote and austere.

119

A photo of someone else's childhood,
a garden in another country—world
he had no part in and has no power to imagine:

yet the old man who has failed his memory
keens over the picture—'Them happy days—
gone—gone for ever!'—glad for a moment to suppose

a focus for unspent grieving, his floating
sense of loss.
He wanders

asking the day of the week, the time,
over and over the wrong questions.
Missing his way in the streets

he acts out
the bent of his life,
the lost way

never looked for, life
unlived, of which he is dying
very slowly.

'A man,'
says his son, 'who never
made a right move in all his life.' A man

who thought **the dollar was sweet** and
couldn't make a buck, riding the subway
year after year to untasted sweetness,

loving his sons obscurely, incurious
who they were, these men, his sons—
a shadow of love, for love longs

to know the beloved, and a light goes with it
into the dark mineshafts of feeling . . . A man
who now, without knowing,

in endless concern for the smallest certainties,
looking again and again at a paid bill,
inquiring again and again, 'When was I here last?'

asks what it's too late to ask:
'Where is my life? Where is my life?
What have I done with my life?'

Who is at my window, who, who?
Go from my window, go, go!
Who calleth there so like a stranger?
Go from my window, go!
J. Wedderburn
1542

Who is at my window, who, who?
It's the blind cuckoo, mulling
the old song over.

The old song is about fear, about
tomorrow and next year.

Timor mortis conturbat me, he sings
What's the use?   He brings me

the image of **when,** a boat
hull down, smudged on the darkening ocean.

I want to move deeper into today;
he keeps me from that work.
Today and eternity are nothing to him.
His wings spread at the window make it dark.

Go from my window, go, go!

As if that hand
squeezing crow's blood
            against a white sky
            beside an idiot's laughing face
were real.

Having set out
in shoes that hurt
by the bog road
            and missed the way.

A cold day
dragging to a
            cold end.

The blood congealing
black
            between the pleased fingers.

In the Japanese
tongue of the
mind's eye one
two syllable word
tells of
the fringe of rain
clinging to the eaves
and of the grey-green
fronds of
wild parsley.

The world is
not with us enough.
O taste and see

the subway Bible poster said,
meaning **The Lord,** meaning
if anything all that lives
to the imagination's tongue,

grief, mercy, language,
tangerine, weather, to
breathe them, bite,
savor, chew, swallow, transform

into our flesh our
deaths, crossing the street, plum, quince,
living in the orchard and being

hungry, and plucking
the fruit.

No skilled hands
caress a stranger's flesh with lucid oil before
a word is spoken
                    no feasting
before a tale is told, before
the stranger tells his name.

The ships come and go
along the river and
in and out of the Narrows
and few among us know it

we are so many

        and many within themselves
travel to far islands but no one
asks for their story

nor is there an exchange of gifts, stranger
        to stranger
nor libation
nor sacrifice to the gods

and no house has its herm.

The river in its abundance
many-voiced
all about us as we stood
on a warm rock to wash

slowly
smoothing in long
              sliding strokes
our soapy hands along each other's
slippery cool bodies

quiet and slow in the midst of
the quick of the
sounding river

our hands were
flames
stealing upon quickened flesh until

no part of us but was
sleek and
on fire

They enter the bare wood, drawn
by a clear-obscure summons they fear
and have no choice but to heed.

A rustling underfoot, a
long trail to go, the thornbushes grow
across the dwindling paths.

Until the small clearing, where they
anticipate violence, knowing some rite
to be performed, and compelled to it.

The man moves forward, the boy
sees what he means to do: from an oaktree
a chain runs at an angle into earth

and they pit themselves to uproot it,
dogged and frightened, to pull the iron
out of the earth's heart.

But from the further depths of the wood
as they strain and weigh on the great chain
appears the spirit,

the wood-demon who summoned them.
And he is not bestial, not fierce
but an old woodsman,

gnarled, shabby, smelling of smoke and sweat,
of a bear's height and shambling like a bear.
Yet his presence is a spirit's presence

and awe takes their breath.
Gentle and rough, laughing a little,
he makes his will known:

not for an act of force he called them,
for no rite of obscure violence
but that they might look about them

and see intricate branch and bark,
stars of moss and the old scars
left by dead men's saws,

and not ask what that chain was.
To leave the open fields
and enter the forest,

that was the rite.
Knowing there was mystery, they could go.
Go back now! And he receded

among the multitude of forms,
the twists and shadows they saw now, listening
to the hum of the world's wood.

Hand of man
hewed from
the mottled rock

almost touching
as Adam the hand of God

smallest inviolate
stone violet

When my body leaves me
I'm lonesome for it.
I've got

eyes, ears,
nose and mouth
and that's all.

Eyes
keep on seeing the
feather blue of the

cold sky,
mouth takes in
hot soup,
nose

smells the frost,

ears hear everything, all
the noises and absences,
but body

goes away to I don't know where
and it's lonesome to drift
above the space it
fills when it's here.

Bricks of the wall,
so much older than the house—
taken I think from a farm pulled down
    when the street was built—
narrow bricks of another century.

Modestly, though laid with panels and parapets,
a wall behind the flowers—
roses and hollyhocks, the silver
pods of lupine, sweet-tasting
phlox, gray
lavender—
      unnoticed—
          but I discovered
the colors in the wall that woke
when spray from the hose
played on its pocks and warts—

a hazy red, a
grain gold, a mauve
of small shadows, sprung
from the quiet dry brown—

          archetype
of the world always a step
beyond the world, that can't
be looked for, only
as the eye wanders,
found.

From the shrivelling gray
silk of its cocoon
a creature slowly
    is pushing out
to stand clear—
           not a butterfly,
             petal that floats at will across
             the summer breeze

           not a furred
           moth of the night
             crusted with indecipherable
             gold—

some primal-shaped, plain-winged, day-flying thing.

Take me or leave me, cries
Melody Grundy. I
like my face.
I am gaily alone.

On my cast-iron horse I was swiftly
everywhere, and no one
saw it for what it was.
That was romance. I leaned

on the mighty tree-stump to watch
an other life at play.
That was joy, I wept, I
leapt into my ship

to sail over grass. Melody
Plenty-of-Friends-Elsewhere
doesn't care,
will sing for all to hear.

Mountain, mountain, mountain,
marking time. Each
nameless, wall beyond wall, wavering
redefinition of
horizon.

And through the months. The arrivals
at dusk in towns one must leave at daybreak

—were they
taken to heart, to be seen
always again,
or let go, those faces,

a door half-open, moss
by matchlight on an inscribed stone?

And by day
through the hours that
rustle about one dryly,
tall grass of the savannah

up to the eyes.
No alternative to the
one-man path.

A wind is blowing. The book being written
shifts, halts, pages
yellow and white drawing apart
and inching together in
new tries. A single white half sheet
skims out under the door.

And cramped in their not yet
halfwritten lives, a man and a woman
grimace in pain. Their cat
yawning its animal secret,
stirs in the monstrous limbo of erasure.
They live (when they live) in fear

of blinding, of burning, of choking under a
mushroom cloud in the year of the roach.
And they want (like us) the eternity
of today, they want this fear to be
struck out at once by a thick black
magic marker, everywhere, every page,

the whole sheets of it crushed, crackling,
and tossed in the fire
            and when they were fine ashes
            the stove would cool and be cleaned
            and a jar of flowers would be put to stand
            on top of the stove in the spring light.

Meanwhile from page to page they
buy things, acquiring the look of a
full life; they argue, make silence bitter,
plan journeys, move house, implant
despair in each other
and then in the nick of time

they save one another with tears,
remorse, tenderness—
hooked on those wonder-drugs.
Yet they do have—
don't they—like us—
their days of grace, they

halt, stretch, a vision
breaks in on the cramped grimace,
inscape of transformation.
Something sundered begins to knit.
By scene, by sentence, something is rendered
back into life, back to the gods.

A form upon the quilted
overcast, gleam, Sacré
Coeur, saltlick
to the mind's
desire—

how shall the pulse
beat out
that measure,
under devious
moon
wander swerving

to wonder—

hands turn
what stone to uncover
feather of broken
oracle—

I slide my face along to the mirror
sideways, to see
that side-smile,
a pale look, tired
and sly. Hey,

who is glancing there?
Shadow-me, not with
malice but mercurially
shot with foreknowledge of
dread and sweat.

Don't lock me in wedlock, I want
marriage, an
encounter—

I told you about the
green light of
May

> (a veil of quiet befallen
> the downtown park,
> late
>
> Saturday after
> noon, long
> shadows and cool
>
> air, scent of
> new grass,
> fresh leaves,
>
> blossom on the threshold of
> abundance—
>
> and the birds I met there,
> birds of passage breaking their journey,
> three birds each of a different species:
>
> the azalea-breasted with round poll, dark,
> the brindled, merry, mousegliding one,
> and the smallest, golden as gorse and wearing
> a black Venetian mask
>
> and with them the three douce hen-birds
> feathered in tender, lively brown—

140

I stood
a half-hour under the enchantment,
no-one passed near,
the birds saw me and

let me be
near them.)

It's not
irrelevant:
I would be
met

and meet you
so,
in a green

airy space, not
locked in.

Hypocrite women, how seldom we speak
of our own doubts, while dubiously
we mother man in his doubt!

And if at Mill Valley perched in the trees
the sweet rain drifting through western air
a white sweating bull of a poet told us

our cunts are ugly—why didn't we
admit we have thought so too? (And
what shame? They are not for the eye!)

No, they are dark and wrinkled and hairy,
caves of the Moon . . .   And when a
dark humming fills us, a

coldness towards life,
we are too much women to
own to such unwomanliness.

Whorishly with the psychopomp
we play and plead—and say
nothing of this later.   And our dreams,

with what frivolity we have pared them
like toenails, clipped them like ends of
split hair.

There's in my mind a woman
of innocence, unadorned but

fair-featured, and smelling of
apples or grass. She wears

a utopian smock or shift, her hair
is light brown and smooth, and she

is kind and very clean without
ostentation—
                but she has
no imagination.
                And there's a
turbulent moon-ridden girl

or old woman, or both,
dressed in opals and rags, feathers

and torn taffeta,
who knows strange songs—

but she is not kind.

Our bodies, still young under
the engraved anxiety of our
faces, and innocently

more expressive than faces:
nipples, navel, and pubic hair
make anyway a

sort of face: or taking
the rounded shadows at
breast, buttock, balls,

the plump of my belly, the
hollow of your
groin, as a constellation,

how it leans from earth to
dawn in a gesture of
play and

wise compassion—
nothing like this
comes to pass
in eyes or wistful
mouths.
        I have

a line or groove I love
runs down
my body from breastbone
to waist. It speaks of
eagerness, of
distance.

Your long back,
the sand color and
how the bones show, say

what sky after sunset
almost white
over a deep woods to which

rooks are homing, says.

Long after you have swung back
away from me
I think you are still with me:

you come in close to the shore
on the tide
and nudge me awake the way

a boat adrift nudges the pier:
am I a pier
half-in half-out of the water?

and in the pleasure of that communion
I lose track,
the moon I watch goes down, the

tide swings you away before
I know I'm
alone again long since,

mud sucking at gray and black
timbers of me,
a light growth of green dreams drying.

At Delphi I prayed
to Apollo
that he maintain in me
the flame of the poem

and I drank of the brackish
spring there, dazed by the
gong beat of the sun,
mistaking it,

as I shrank from the eagle's
black shadow crossing
that sky of cruel blue,
for the Pierian Spring—

and soon after
vomited my moussaka
and then my guts writhed
for some hours with diarrhea

until at dusk
among the stones of the goatpaths
breathing dust
I questioned my faith, or

within it wondered
if the god mocked me.
But since then, though it flickers or
shrinks to a

blue bead on the wick,
there's that in me that
burns and chills, blackening
my heart with its soot,

flaring in laughter, stinging
my feet into a dance, so that
I think sometimes not Apollo heard me
but a different god.

Certain branches cut
certain leaves fallen
the grapes
           cooked and put up
for winter

mountains without one
shrug of cloud
no feint of blurred
wind-willow leaf-light

their chins up
in blue of the eastern sky
their red cloaks
wrapped tight to the bone

Let me walk through the fields of paper
touching with my wand
dry stems and stunted
butterflies—

let Sluggard Acre send up
sunflowers among its weeds,
ten foot high—let its thistles
display their Scottish magnificence,
mauve tam-o'-shanters and barbed plaids—

yes, set fire to frostbitten crops,
drag out forgotten fruit
to dance the flame-tango,
the smoke-gavotte,
to live after all—

let the note **elephant** become a song,
the white beast wiser than man
raise a dust in the north woods,
loping on corduroy roads to the arena.

> '. . . in those wine- and urine-stained
> hallways, something in me won-
> dered, *What will happen to all that
> black beauty?*'
>   *James Baldwin*

Out of those hallways
crossing the street to blue
astonished eyes

as though by first light
made visible, dark
presences slowly
focus

revelation of
tulip blacks, delicate
browns, proportion
of heavy lip to bevelled
temple bone

          The mind
of a fair man at the intersection
jars
at the entering of this
beauty, filing

endlessly through his blue
blinking eyes into
the world within him

I could replace
God for awhile, that old ring of candles,
that owl's wing brushing the dew
off my grass hair.
If bended knee calls up
a god, if the imagination of idol
calls up a god, if melting
of heart or what was written as
bowels but has to do
                 not with shit but with salutation of
                 somber beauty in what is mortal,
calls up a god by recognition and power of
longing, then in my forest
God is replaced awhile,
awhile I can turn from that slow embrace
to worship *mortal*, the summoned
god who has speech, who has wit
to wreathe all words, who laughs
wrapped in sad pelt and without hope of heaven,
who makes a music turns the heads
of all beasts
as mine turns, dream-hill grass
standing on end at echo even.

There are weeds that flower forth in fall
in a gray cloud of seed that seems
from a not so great distance
plumblossom, pearblossom,
or first snow,

as if in a fog of feather-light
goosedown-silvery seed-thoughts
a rusty mind in its autumn
reviewed, renewed
its winged power.

My great brother
         Lord of the Song
wears the ruff of
         forest bear.

Husband, thy fleece of silk is black,
         a black adornment;
lies so close to the turns of the flesh,
burns my palm-stroke.

My great brother
         Lord of the Song
wears the ruff of
         forest bear.

Strong legs of our son are dusted
         dark with hair.
Told of long roads,
we know his stride.

My great brother
         Lord of the Song
wears the ruff of
         forest bear.

Hair of man, man-hair, hair of
breast and groin, marking contour as
     silverpoint marks in cross-
     hatching, as river-
         grass on the woven current
         indicates ripple,
praise.

*(These words were given me in a
dream. In the dream I was a Finnish
child of 8 or 9 who had been given
by her teacher the task of writing
out these 3 ancient runes of her
people. This is how they went:)*

(1) Know the pinetrees. Know the orange dryness of sickness
and death in needle and cone. Know them too in green health,
those among whom your life is laid.

(2) Know the ship you sail on. Know its timbers. Deep the
fjord waters where you sail, steep the cliffs, deep into the un-
known coast goes the winding fjord. But what would you
have? Would you be tied up to a sandwhite quay in perpetual
sunshine, yards and masts sprouting little violet mandolins?

(3) In city, in suburb, in forest, no way to stretch out the
arms— so if you would grow, go straight up or deep down.

THE SORROW DANCE (1967)

I   ABEL'S BRIDE

Something hangs in back of me,
I can't see it, can't move it.

I know it's black,
a hump on my back.

It's heavy. You
can't see it.

What's in it? Don't tell me
you don't know. It's

what you told me about—
black

inimical power, cold
whirling out of it and

around me and
sweeping you flat.

But what if,
like a camel, it's

pure energy I store,
and carry humped and heavy?

Not black, not
that terror, stupidity

of cold rage; or black
only for being pent there?

What if released in air
it became a white

source of light, a fountain
of light? Could all that weight

be the power of flight?
Look inward: see me

with embryo wings, one
feathered in soot, the other

blazing ciliations of ember, pale
flare-pinions. Well—

could I go
on one wing,

the white one?

Woman fears for man, he goes
out alone to his labors. No mirror
nests in his pocket. His face
opens and shuts with his hopes.
His sex hangs unhidden
or rises before him
blind and questing.

She thinks herself
lucky. But sad. When she goes out
she looks in the glass, she remembers
herself. Stones, coal,
the hiss of water upon the kindled
branches—her being
is a cave, there are bones at the hearth.

A nervous smile as gaze meets
gaze across
deep
river.
What place
for a smile here;
         it edges away

leaves us each at ravine's edge
alone with our bodies.

We plunge—
O dark river!
towards each other—
into that element—

a deep fall,
the eyes closing as if forever,
the air ripping, the waters
cleaving and closing upon us.

Heavy we are, our flesh
of stone and velvet goes down,
goes down.

What is green in me
darkens, muscadine.

If woman is inconstant,
good, I am faithful to

ebb and flow, I fall
in season and now

is a time of ripening.
If her part

is to be true,
a north star,

good, I hold steady
in the black sky

and vanish by day,
yet burn there

in blue or above
quilts of cloud.

There is no savor
more sweet, more salt

than to be glad to be
what, woman,

and who, myself,
I am, a shadow

that grows longer as the sun
moves, drawn out

on a thread of wonder.
If I bear burdens

they begin to be remembered
as gifts, goods, a basket

of bread that hurts
my shoulders but closes me

in fragrance. I can
eat as I go.

We are a meadow where the bees hum,
mind and body are almost one

as the fire snaps in the stove
and our eyes close,

and mouth to mouth, the covers
pulled over our shoulders,

we drowse as horses drowse afield,
in accord; though the fall cold

surrounds our warm bed, and though
by day we are singular and often lonely.

i   **The Disclosure**

He-who-came-forth was
it turned out
a man—

Moves among us from room to room of our life
in boots, in jeans, in a cloak of flame
pulled out of his pocket along with
old candywrappers, where it had lain
transferred from pants to pants,
folded small as a curl of dust,
from the beginning—

unfurled now.

The fine flame
almost unseen in common light.

ii   **The Woodblock**

He cuts into a slab of wood,
engrossed, violently precise.
Thus, yesterday, the day before yesterday,
engines of fantasy were evolved
in poster paints. Tonight
a face forms under the knife,

slashed with stern
crisscrosses of longing, downstrokes
of silence endured—
                    his visioned
own face!—
down which from one eye

rolls a tear.
            His own face
drawn from the wood,

deep in the manhood his childhood
so swiftly led to, a small brook rock-leaping
into the rapt, imperious, seagoing river.

'Living a life'—
the beauty of deep lines
dug in your cheeks.

The years gather by sevens
to fashion you. They are blind,
but you are not blind.

Their blows resound,
they are deaf, those laboring
daughters of the Fates,

but you are not deaf,
you pick out
your own song from the uproar

line by line,
and at last throw back
your head and sing it.

Hymn to Eros

O Eros, silently smiling one, hear me.
Let the shadow of thy wings
brush me.
Let thy presence
enfold me, as if darkness
were swandown.
Let me see that darkness
lamp in hand,
this country become
the other country
sacred to desire.

Drowsy god,
slow the wheels of my thought
so that I listen only
to the snowfall hush of
thy circling.
Close my beloved with me
in the smoke ring of thy power,
that we may be, each to the other,
figures of flame,
figures of smoke,
figures of flesh
newly seen in the dusk.

II   THE EARTH WORM

Making it, making it,
in their chosen field
the roses fall
victim to a weakness of the heart.

Scoring
so high
no one counts the cost.
The blue moon
light on their profusion darkens.

The worm artist
out of soil, by passage
of himself
constructing.
Castles of metaphor!
Delicate
       dungeon turrets!
He throws off
artifacts as he
contracts and expands the
muscle of his being,
ringed in himself,
tilling. He
is homage to
earth, aerates
the ground of his living.

The Unknown

for Muriel Rukeyser

The kettle changes its note,
the steam sublimed.

Supererogatory divinations one is
lured on by!
     The routine
is decent. As if the white page
were a clean tablecloth,
as if the vacuumed floor were
a primed canvas, as if
new earrings made from old shells
of tasty abalone were nose rings for the two most beautiful
girls of a meticulous island, whose bodies are oiled as one oils
a table of teak . . . Hypocrisies
of seemly hope, performed to make a place
for miracles to occur; and if the day
is no day for miracles, then the preparations
are an order one may rest in.

       But one doesn't want
rest, one wants miracles. Each time that note
changes (which is whenever you let it)—the kettle
(already boiling) passing into enlightenment without
a moment's pause, out of fury into
quiet praise—desire
wakes again. *Begin over.*

It is to hunt a white deer
in snowy woods. Beaten
you fall asleep in the afternoon
on a sofa.
And wake to witness,
softly backing away from you, mollified,
all that the room had insisted on—
eager furniture, differentiated planes. . .
Twilight has come, the windows
are big and solemn, brimful of the afterglow;
and sleep has swept through the mind, loosening
brown leaves from their twigs to drift
out of sight
beyond the horizon's black rooftops.
A winter's dirt
makes Indian silk squares of the windowpanes,
semi transparent, a designed
middle distance.
The awakening is
to transformation,
word after word.

Brown and silver, the tufted
rushes hold sway
by the Hackensack

and small sunflowers
freckled with soot
clamber out of the fill

in gray haze of
Indian summer
among the paraphernalia

of oil refineries, the crude
industrial débris,
leftover shacks

rusting under dark
wings of Skyway—

tenacious dreamers
sifting the wind
day and night, their roots

in seeping waters—

and fierce in each disk
of coarse yellow the archaic
smile, almost
agony, almost

a boy's grin.

The flowerlike
animal perfume
in the god's curly
hair—

don't assume
that like a flower's
his attributes
are there to tempt

you or
direct the moth's
hunger—
simply he is
the temple of himself,

hair and hide
a sacrifice of blood and flowers
on his altar

if any worshipper
kneel or not.

III   THE CRUST

Joy

You must love the crust of the earth
on which you dwell. You must be
able to extract nutriment out of a
sandheap. You must have so good
an appetite as this, else you will live
in vain.

Thoreau

Joy, the, 'well . . . *joyfulness* of
joy'—'many years
I had not known it,' the woman of eighty
said, 'only remembered, till now.'

Traherne
in dark fields.
           On Tremont Street,
on the Common, a raw dusk, Emerson
'glad to the brink of fear.'
           It is objective,

stands founded, a roofed gateway;
we cloud-wander

away from it, stumble
again towards it not seeing it,

enter cast-down, discover ourselves
'in joy' as 'in love.'

ii

         'They knocked an
old scar off—the pent blood
rivered out and out—
         When I

white and weak, understood what befell me

speech quickened in me, I
came to myself,'
         —a poet
fifty years old, her look a pool
whose sands have down-spiralled, each grain

dream-clear now, the water
freely itself, visible transparence.

iii

Seeing the locus of joy as the gate
of a city, or as a lych-gate,

I looked up lych-gate: it means
body-gate—here the bearers

rested the bier till the priest came
(to ferry it into a new world).
         'You bring me

life!' Rilke cried to his
deathbed visitor; then, 'Help me

towards my death,' then, 'Never forget,
dear one, life is
magnificent!'
            I looked up 'Joy'
in *Origins,* and came to

'Jubilation' that goes back
to 'a cry of joy or woe' or to 'echoic
iu of wonder.'

iv

Again the old lady
sure for the first time there is a term
to her earth-life

enters the gate—'Joy is
so special a thing, vivid—'

her love for the earth
returns, her heart lightens,
she savors the crust.

Animal willows of November
in pelt of gold enduring when all else
has let go all ornament
and stands naked in the cold.
Cold shine of sun on swamp water,
cold caress of slant beam on bough,
gray light on brown bark.
Willows—last to relinquish a leaf,
curious, patient, lion-headed, tense
with energy, watching
the serene cold through a curtain
of tarnished strands.

Arbor vitae, whose grooved bole
reveals so many broken
intentions, branches
lopped or
wizened off,

in the grass near you
your scions are uprising,
fernlike, trustful.

The young elm that must be cut
because its roots push at the house wall

taps and scrapes my window
urgently—but when I look round at it

remains still. Or if I turn by chance,
it seems its leaves are eyes, or the whole spray
of leaves and twigs a face flattening
its nose against the glass, breathing a cloud,

longing to see clearly my life whose term
is not yet known.

Annuals

('Plants that flower the first season
the seed is sown, and then die')

All I planted came up,
balsam and nasturtium and
cosmos and the Marvel of Peru

first the cotyledon
then thickly the differentiated
true leaves of the seedlings,

and I transplanted them,
carefully shaking out each one's
hairfine rootlets from the earth,

and they have thriven,
well-watered in the new-turned earth;
and grow apace now—

but not one shows signs of a flower,
not one.
          If August passes
flowerless,
and the frosts come,

will I have learned to rejoice enough
in the sober wonder of
green healthy leaves?

189

The cat on my bosom
sleeping and purring
—fur-petalled chrysanthemum,
squirrel-killer—

is a metaphor only if I
force him to be one,
looking too long in his pale, fond,
dilating, contracting eyes

that reject mirrors, refuse
to observe what bides
stockstill.
           Likewise

flex and reflex of claws
gently pricking through sweater to skin
gently sustains their own tune,
not mine. I-Thou, cat, I-Thou.

When to my melancholy
All is folly
   then the whirr
of the hummingbird
at intervals throughout the day

is all that's sure
to stir me, makes me
jump up, scattering

papers, books, pens—
    To the bay window,
and certainly

there he is below it
true-aimed at the minute cups of
Coral Bells, swerving

perfectly,
the fierce, brilliant faith
that pierces the heart all summer

and sips bitter insects steeped in nectar,
prima materia
of gleam-and-speed-away.

A passion so intense
It driveth sorrow hence. . .

IV   THE SORROW DANCE

A headless squirrel, some blood
oozing from the unevenly
chewed-off neck

lies in rainsweet grass
near the woodshed door.
Down the driveway

the first irises
have opened since dawn,
ethereal, their mauve

almost a transparent gray,
their dark veins
bruise-blue.

Those groans men use
passing a woman on the street
or on the steps of the subway

to tell her she is a female
and their flesh knows it,

are they a sort of tune,
an ugly enough song, sung
by a bird with a slit tongue

but meant for music?

Or are they the muffled roaring
of deafmutes trapped in a building that is
slowly filling with smoke?

Perhaps both.

Such men most often
look as if groan were all they could do,
yet a woman, in spite of herself,

knows it's a tribute:
if she were lacking all grace
they'd pass her in silence:

so it's not only to say she's
a warm hole. It's a word

in grief-language, nothing to do with
primitive, not an ur-language;
language stricken, sickened, cast down

in decrepitude. She wants to
throw the tribute away, dis-
gusted, and can't,

it goes on buzzing in her ear,
it changes the pace of her walk,
the torn posters in echoing corridors

spell it out, it
quakes and gnashes as the train comes in.
Her pulse sullenly

had picked up speed,
but the cars slow down and
jar to a stop while her understanding

keeps on translating:
'Life after life after life goes by

without poetry,
without seemliness,
without love.'

In world, world
of terror,
filling up fast with
unintelligible
signs:

imploring pinkpalmed hand
twitching, autonomous,
hung from an ordinary
black arm
        (the lights change,
          it's gone)

wind
skirting the
clots of spittle,
smears of
dogshit, pushing

shadows of unknown
objects across and
away and
half across the
sidewalks, arhythmic.

The impasto of what is past,
the purple!
        Avalanches
of swarthy yellow!
              But the unremembered
makes itself into a granite-hued
nylon scarf, tight at the throat—
flies out
        backwards, a drifting
banner, tangles
the wheel.

In a landscape of boxed interiors,
among clefts, revealed strata, roofed-over
shafts, the road roves.
             A shadow

not of a bird, not of a cloud,
draws a dark stroke over
the hills, the mind.
And another, another.
Our fears keep pace with us.
We are driven.
We drive

on, shift gears, grind
up into the present in first, stop,
look out, look down.
In dust
        the lace designs incised

by feet of beetles:
paths crossing, searching—
here a broad swathe
where manna was found, and dragged
away to be savored.
                              At the horizon

flowers
vaster than cathedrals
are crowding. The motor idles.
Over the immense upland
the pulse of their blossoming
thunders through us.

As It Happens

Like dogs in Mexico,
furless, sore, misshapen,

arrives from laborious nowhere
Agony. And proves

to have eyes of kindness,
a pitiful tail; wants

love. Give it some, in form of
dry tortilla, it

grabs and runs off
three-leggéd, scared,

but tarries nearby and will
return. A friend.

Grief, have I denied thee?
Grief, I have denied thee.

That robe or tunic, black gauze
over black and silver my sister wore
to dance *Sorrow*, hung so long
in my closet. I never tried it on.
        And my dance
was *Summer*—they rouged my cheeks
and twisted roses with wire stems into my hair.
I was compliant, Juno de sept ans,
betraying my autumn birthright pour faire plaisir.
Always denial. Grief in the morning, washed away
in coffee, crumbled to a dozen errands between
busy fingers.

        Or across cloistral shadow, insistent
intrusion of pink sunstripes from open
archways, falling recurrent.

Corrosion denied, the figures the acid designs
filled in. Grief dismissed,
and Eros along with grief.
Phantasmagoria swept across the sky
by shaky winds endlessly,
the spaces of blue timidly steady—
blue curtains at trailer windows framing
the cinder walks.
There are hidden corners of sky
choked with the swept shreds, with pain and ashes.
                        Grief,

have I denied thee? Denied thee.
The emblems torn from the walls,
and the black plumes.

202

(*Olga Levertoff, 1914–1964*)

i

By the gas-fire, kneeling
to undress,
scorching luxuriously, raking
her nails over olive sides, the red
waistband ring—

(And the little sister
beady-eyed in the bed—
or drowsy, was I? My head
a camera—)

Sixteen. Her breasts
round, round, and
dark-nippled—

who now these two months long
is bones and tatters of flesh in earth.

ii

The high pitch of
nagging insistence, lines
creased into raised brows—

Ridden, ridden—
the skin around the nails
nibbled sore—

You wanted
to shout the world to its senses,
did you?—to browbeat

the poor into joy's
socialist republic—
What rage

and human shame swept you
when you were nine and saw
the Ley Street houses,

grasping their meaning as *slum*.
Where I, reaching that age,
teased you, admiring

architectural probity, circa
eighteen-fifty, and noted
pride in the whitened doorsteps.

Black one, black one,
there was a white
candle in your heart.

iii

i

Everything flows
              she muttered into my childhood,
pacing the trampled grass where human puppets
rehearsed fates that summer,
stung into alien semblances by the lash of her will—

everything flows—
I looked up from my Littlest Bear's cane armchair
and knew the words came from a book
and felt them alien to me

but linked to words we loved
                              from the hymnbook—*Time*
like an ever-rolling stream / bears all its sons away—

ii

Now as if smoke or sweetness were blown my way
I inhale a sense of her livingness in that instant,
feeling, dreaming, hoping, knowing boredom and zest like anyone
                                                          else—
a young girl in the garden, the same alchemical square
I grew in, we thought sometimes
too small for our grand destinies—
                              But dread
was in her, a bloodbeat, it was against the rolling dark
oncoming river she raised bulwarks, setting herself
to sift cinders after early Mass all of one winter,

labelling her desk's normal disorder, basing
her verses on Keble's *Christian Year*, picking
those endless arguments, pressing on

to manipulate lives to disaster . . . To change,
to change the course of the river! What rage for order
disordered her pilgrimage—so that for years at a time

she would hide among strangers, waiting
to rearrange all mysteries in a new light.

Black one, incubus—
    she appeared
riding anguish as Tartars ride mares

over the stubble of bad years.

In one of the years
    when I didn't know if she were dead or alive
I saw her in dream

haggard and rouged
        lit by the flare
from an eel- or cockle-stand on a slum street—

was it a dream? I had lost

all sense, almost, of
    who she was, what—inside of her skin,
under her black hair
             dyed blonde—

it might feel like to be, in the wax and wane of the moon,
in the life I feel as unfolding, not flowing, the pilgrim years—

iv

On your hospital bed you lay
in love, the hatreds
that had followed you, a
comet's tail, burned out

as your disasters bred of love
burned out,
while pain and drugs
quarreled like sisters in you—

lay afloat on a sea
of love and pain—how you always
loved that cadence, 'Underneath
are the everlasting arms'—

all history
burned out, down
to the sick bone, save for

that kind candle.

v

i

In a garden grene whenas I lay—

you set the words to a tune so plaintive
it plucks its way through my life as through a wood.

As through a wood, shadow and light between birches,
gliding a moment in open glades, hidden by thickets of holly

your life winds in me.   In Valentines
a root protrudes from the greensward several yards from its tree

we might raise like a trapdoor's handle, you said,
and descend long steps to another country

where we would live without father or mother
and without longing for the upper world. *The birds
sang sweet,* O song, *in the midst of the daye,*

and we entered silent mid-Essex churches on hot afternoons
and communed with the effigies of knights and their ladies

and their slender dogs asleep at their feet,
the stone so cold—   *In youth*

is pleasure, in youth is pleasure.

ii

Under autumn clouds, under white
wideness of winter skies you went walking
the year you were most alone

returning to the old roads, seeing again
the signposts pointing to Theydon Garnon
or Stapleford Abbots or Greensted,

crossing the ploughlands (whose color I named *murple,*
a shade between brown and mauve that we loved
when I was a child and you

not much more than a child) finding new lanes
near White Roding or Abbess Roding; or lost in Romford's
new streets where there were footpaths then—

frowning as you ground out your thoughts, breathing deep
of the damp still air, taking
the frost into your mind unflinching.

How cold it was in your thin coat, your down-at-heel shoes—
tearless Niobe, your children were lost to you
and the stage lights had gone out, even the empty theater

was locked to you, cavern of transformation where all
had almost been possible.
                              How many books
you read in your silent lodgings that winter,
how the plovers transpierced your solitude out of doors with their
                                                        strange cries
I had flung open my arms to in longing, once, by your side
stumbling over the furrows—

Oh, in your torn stockings, with unwaved hair,
you were trudging after your anguish
over the bare fields, soberly, soberly.

vi

Your eyes were the brown gold of pebbles under water.
I never crossed the bridge over the Roding, dividing
the open field of the present from the mysteries,
the wraiths and shifts of time-sense Wanstead Park held suspended,
without remembering your eyes. Even when we were estranged
and my own eyes smarted in pain and anger at the thought of you.
And by other streams in other countries; anywhere where the light
reaches down through shallows to gold gravel. Olga's
brown eyes. One rainy summer, down in the New Forest,
when we could hardly breathe for ennui and the low sky,
you turned savagely to the piano and sightread
straight through all the Beethoven sonatas, day after day—
weeks, it seemed to me. I would turn the pages some of the time,
go out to ride my bike, return—you were enduring in the

falls and rapids of the music, the arpeggios rang out, the rectory
trembled, our parents seemed effaced.
I think of your eyes in that photo, six years before I was born,
the fear in them. What did you do with your fear,
later? Through the years of humiliation,
of paranoia and blackmail and near-starvation, losing
the love of those you loved, one after another,
parents, lovers, children, idolized friends, what kept
compassion's candle alight in you, that lit you
clear into another chapter (but the same book) 'a clearing
in the selva oscura,
a house whose door
swings open, a hand beckons
in welcome'?
                    I cross
so many brooks in the world, there is so much light
dancing on so many stones, so many questions my eyes
smart to ask of your eyes, gold brown eyes,
the lashes short but the lids
arched as if carved out of olivewood, eyes with some vision
of festive goodness in back of their hard, or veiled, or shining,
unknowable gaze. . .

May–August, 1964

NOTE: The quoted lines in the sixth section are an adapta-
tion of some lines in 'Selva Oscura' by the late Louis Mac-
Neice, a poem much loved by my sister.

210

Ugly look, close to tears, on a man's face—
    hath compassion
    no name for it?
Look not unlike a fearful animal's
snarl as the hunter backs him up,
    but here
    no bite showing,
    the lips drawn down not back.

Drawn down, sweet lips
    of a man
as if Laurel were about
to cry—compassion
    turns in on itself
biting its tongue, unable to cry out
    or give it a name.

The Closed World

'If the Perceptive Organs close, their
Objects seem to close also.'
                              Blake: *Jerusalem*

The house-snake dwells here still
under the threshold
but for months I have not seen it
nor its young, the inheritors.

Light and the wind enact
passion and resurrection
day in, day out
but the blinds are down over my windows,
my doors are shut.

When after the long drought at last
silver and darkness swept over the hills
the dry indifferent glare in my mind's eye
wavered but burned on.

To speak of sorrow
works upon it
              moves it from its
crouched place barring
the way to and from the soul's hall—

out in the light it
shows clear, whether
shrunken or known as
a giant wrath—
              discrete
at least, where before

its great shadow joined
the walls and roof and seemed
to uphold the hall like a beam.

V   PERSPECTIVES

Let me be at the place of the castle.
Let the castle be within me.
Let it rise foursquare from the moat's ring.
Let the moat's waters reflect green plumage of ducks, let
the shells of swimming turtles break the surface or be
seen through the rippling depths.
Let horsemen be stationed at the rim of it, and a dog, al-
ways alert on the brink of sleep.
Let the space under the first storey be dark, let the water
lap the stone posts, and vivid green slime glimmer
upon them; let a boat be kept there.
Let the caryatids of the second storey be bears upheld on
beams that are dragons.
On the parapet of the central room, let there be four arch-
ers, looking off to the four horizons. Within, let the
prince be at home, let him sit in deep thought, at
peace, all the windows open to the loggias.
Let the young queen sit above, in the cool air, her child in
her arms; let her look with joy at the great circle, the
pilgrim shadows, the work of the sun and the play of
the wind. Let her walk to and fro. Let the columns
uphold the roof, let the storeys uphold the columns,
let there be dark space below the lowest floor, let the
castle rise foursquare out of the moat, let the moat be a
ring and the water deep, let the guardians guard it, let
there be wide lands around it, let that country where it
stands be within me, let me be where it is.

The dawn alps,
the stilled snake of
river asleep in its
wide bed,

'to exemplify something we desire in our
own nature.'

Or six miles down
below our hawkstill swiftness

                              the sea
                              wakening.

And when we
come to earth the roofs
are made of tiles,
pigeons
are walking on them,

little bushes
become shade trees.

The Postcards: A Triptych

The Minoan Snake Goddess is flanked by a Chardin still-life, somber
and tranquil, and by Mohammedan angels
brilliantly clothed and with multicolored wings,
who throng round a fleshcolored horse with a man's face
on whose back rides a white-turbanned being without a face,
merely a white, oval disk, and whose hands too are unformed, or
hidden
in blue sleeves.
                    Are the angels bringing attributes
          to this unconscious one?
Is he about to be made human?
                              One bends to the floor of heaven in
                                        prayer;
one brings a bowl (of water?) another a tray (of food?); two
point the way, one watches from on high, two and two more
indicate measure, that is, they present
limits that confine the way to a single path;
two debate the outcome, the last
prays not bowed down but looking
level towards the pilgrim.
Stars and the winding
ceintures of the angels surround
the gold cloud or flame before which he rides; heaven itself
is a dark blue.
                    Meanwhile the still-life offers, makes possible,
a glass of water, a wine-bottle made of glass so dark it is
almost black yet not opaque, half full of
perhaps water; and beside these, two courgettes
with rough, yellow-green, almost reptilian skins,
          and a shallow basket
of plums, each almost cleft
with ripeness, the bloom upon them, their skin
darker purple or almost crimson where a hand
touched them, placing them here. Surely

219

this table, these fruits, these vessels, this water
stand in a cool room, stonefloored, quiet.
And the Goddess?
                              She stands
between the worlds.
                              She is ivory,
her breast bare, her bare arms
braceleted with gold snakes. Their heads
uprear towards her in homage.
Gold borders the tiers of her skirt, a gold hoop
is locked round her waist. She is a few inches high.
And she muses, her lips are pursed,
beneath her crown that must once have been studded with gold
she frowns, she gazes
at and beyond her snakes as if
not goddess but priestess, waiting
an augury.
                    Without thought I have placed these images
over my desk. Under these signs
I am living.

How I woke to the color-tone
as of peach-juice
dulcet bells were
tolling.
        And how my pleasure
was in the strength of my back,
in my noble shoulders, the cool
smooth flesh cylinders of my arms.
How I seemed a woman tall and
full-rounded, ready
to step into daylight sound as a bell

but continued to awake
further, and found myself
myself, smaller,
not thin but thinner, nervous,
who hurries without animal calm.
And how the sweet
blur of the bells

lapsed, and ceased,
and it was not morning.

The killings continue, each second
pain and misfortune extend themselves
in the genetic chain, injustice is done knowingly, and the air
bears the dust of decayed hopes,
yet breathing those fumes, walking the thronged
pavements among crippled lives, jackhammers
raging, a parking lot painfully agleam
in the May sun, I have seen
not behind but within, within the
dull grief, blown grit, hideous
concrete façades, another grief, a gleam
as of dew, an abode of mercy,
have heard not behind but within noise
a humming that drifted into a quiet smile.
Nothing was changed, all was revealed otherwise;
not that horror was not, not that the killings did not continue,
not that I thought there was to be no more despair,
but that as if transparent all disclosed
an otherness that was blessèd, that was bliss.
I saw Paradise in the dust of the street.

A Vision

'The intellectual love of a thing is
the understanding of its perfections.'
Spinoza, quoted by Ezra Pound

Two angels among the throng of angels
paused in the upward abyss,
facing angel to angel.

Blue and green glowed the wingfeathers
of one angel, from red to gold the sheen
of the other's. These two,

so far as angels may dispute, were poised
on the brink of dispute, brink of
fall from angelic stature,

for these tall ones, angels
whose wingspan encompasses entire
earthly villages, whose heads if their feet touched earth

would top pines or redwoods, live by their vision's harmony
which sees at one glance
the dark and light of the moon.

These two hovered dazed before one another,
for one saw the seafeathered, peacock breakered
crests of the other angel's magnificence,
different from his own,

and the other's eyes flickered with vision of
flame petallings, cream-gold grainfeather glitterings,
the wings of his fellow,

223

and both in immortal danger of dwindling, of dropping
into the remote forms of a lesser being.

But as these angels, the only halted ones
among the many who passed and repassed,
trod air as swimmers tread water, each gazing

on the angelic wings of the other,
the intelligence proper to great angels flew into their wings,
the intelligence called *intellectual love,* which,
understanding the perfections of scarlet,

leapt up among blues and greens strongshafted,
and among amber down illumined the sapphire bloom,

so that each angel was iridescent with the strange newly-seen
hues he watched; and their discovering pause
and the speech their silent interchange of perfection was

never became a shrinking to opposites,

and they remained free in the heavenly chasm,
remained angels, but dreaming angels,
each imbued with the mysteries of the other.

VI   LIFE AT WAR

The Pulse

Sealed inside the anemone
in the dark, I knock my head
on steel petals
curving inward around me.

Somewhere the edict is given:
petals, relax.
Delicately they arch over backward.
All is opened to me—

the air they call *water*,
saline, dawngreen over its sands,
resplendent with fishes.
All day it is morning,

all night the glitter
of all that shines out of itself
crisps the vast swathes of the current.
But my feet are weighted:

only my seafern arms
my human hands
my fingers tipped with fire
sway out into the world.

Fair is the world.
I sing. The ache
up from heel to knee
of the weights

gives to the song its
ground bass.
And before the song
attains even a first refrain

the petals creak and
begin to rise.
They rise and recurl
to a bud's form

and clamp shut.
I wait in the dark.

The disasters numb within us
caught in the chest, rolling
in the brain like pebbles. The feeling
resembles lumps of raw dough

weighing down a child's stomach on baking day.
Or Rilke said it, 'My heart. . .
Could I say of it, it overflows
with bitterness . . . but no, as though

its contents were simply balled into
formless lumps, thus
do I carry it about.'
The same war

continues.
We have breathed the grits of it in, all our lives,
our lungs are pocked with it,
the mucous membrane of our dreams
coated with it, the imagination
filmed over with the gray filth of it:

the knowledge that humankind,

delicate Man, whose flesh
responds to a caress, whose eyes
are flowers that perceive the stars,

whose music excels the music of birds,
whose laughter matches the laughter of dogs,
whose understanding manifests designs
fairer than the spider's most intricate web,

still turns without surprise, with mere regret
to the scheduled breaking open of breasts whose milk
runs out over the entrails of still-alive babies,
transformation of witnessing eyes to pulp-fragments,
implosion of skinned penises into carcass-gulleys.

We are the humans, men who can make;
whose language imagines *mercy,*
lovingkindness; we have believed one another
mirrored forms of a God we felt as good—

who do these acts, who convince ourselves
it is necessary; these acts are done
to our own flesh; burned human flesh
is smelling in Viet Nam as I write.

Yes, this is the knowledge that jostles for space
in our bodies along with all we
go on knowing of joy, of love;

our nerve filaments twitch with its presence
day and night,
nothing we say has not the husky phlegm of it in the saying,
nothing we do has the quickness, the sureness,
the deep intelligence living at peace would have.

The blood we give the dead to drink
is deeds we do at the will of the dead spirits in us,
not our own live will.
The dead who thirst to speak
had no good of words or deeds when they lived,
or not enough, and were left in longing.
Their longing to speak, their thirst
for the blood of their deeds done by us,
would leave no time, place, force,
for our own deeds, our own
imagination of speech.
Refuse them!
If we too miss out, don't create our lives,
invent our deeds, do them, dance
a tune with our own feet,
we shall thirst in Hades,
in the blood of our children.

Second Didactic Poem

The honey of man is
the task we're set to: to be
'more ourselves'
in the making:
            'bees of the invisible' working
in cells of flesh and psyche,
filling
        'la grande ruche d'or.'

Nectar,
        the makings of the
incorruptible,
            is carried upon the
corrupt tongues of
mortal insects,
fanned with their wisps of wing
                'to evaporate
excess water,'
                enclosed and capped
with wax, the excretion
of bees' abdominal glands.
Beespittle, droppings, hairs
of beefur: all become honey.
Virulent micro-organisms cannot
survive in honey.
                The taste,
the odor of honey:
each has no analogue but itself.

232

In our gathering, in our containing, in our
working, active within ourselves,
slowly the pale
dew-beads of light
lapped up from flowers
can thicken,
darken to gold:

honey of the human.

1) Did the people of Viet Nam
   use lanterns of stone?
2) Did they hold ceremonies
   to reverence the opening of buds?
3) Were they inclined to quiet laughter?
4) Did they use bone and ivory,
   jade and silver, for ornament?
5) Had they an epic poem?
6) Did they distinguish between speech and singing?

1) Sir, their light hearts turned to stone.
   It is not remembered whether in gardens
   stone lanterns illumined pleasant ways.
2) Perhaps they gathered once to delight in blossom,
   but after the children were killed
   there were no more buds.
3) Sir, laughter is bitter to the burned mouth.
4) A dream ago, perhaps. Ornament is for joy.
   All the bones were charred.
5) It is not remembered. Remember,
   most were peasants; their life
   was in rice and bamboo.
   When peaceful clouds were reflected in the paddies
   and the water buffalo stepped surely along terraces,
   maybe fathers told their sons old tales.
   When bombs smashed those mirrors
   there was time only to scream.
6) There is an echo yet
   of their speech which was like a song.
   It was reported their singing resembled
   the flight of moths in moonlight.
   Who can say? It is silent now.

Two Variations

i Enquiry

You who go out on schedule
to kill, do you know
there are eyes that watch you,
eyes whose lids you burned off,
that see you eat your steak
and buy your girlflesh
and sell your PX goods
and sleep?
She is not old,
she whose eyes
know you.
She will outlast you.
She saw
her five young children
writhe and die;
in that hour
she began to watch you,
she whose eyes are open forever.

ii The Seeing

Hands over my eyes I see
blood and the little bones;
or when a blanket covers
the sockets I see the
weave; at night the glare softens
but I have power now
to see there is only gray
on gray, the sleepers, the
altar. I see the living
and the dead; the dead are

as if alive, the mouth of
my youngest son pulls my
breast, but there is no milk, he
is a ghost; through his flesh
I see the dying of those
said to be alive, they
eat rice and speak to me but
I see dull death in them
and while they speak I see
myself on my mat, body
and eyes, eyes that see a
hand in the unclouded sky,
a human hand, release
wet fire, the rain that gave
my eyes their vigilance.

The Altars in the Street

On June 17th, 1966, The New York Times
reported that, as part of the Buddhist cam-
paign of non-violent resistance, Viet-Namese
children were building altars in the streets
of Saigon and Hue, effectively jamming
traffic.

Children begin at green dawn nimbly to build
topheavy altars, overweighted with prayers,
thronged each instant more densely

with almost-visible ancestors.
Where tanks have cracked the roadway
the frail altars shake; here a boy

with red stumps for hands steadies a corner,
here one adjusts with his crutch the holy base.
The vast silence of Buddha overtakes

and overrules the oncoming roar
of tragic life that fills alleys and avenues;
it blocks the way of pedicabs, police, convoys.

The hale and maimed together
hurry to construct for the Buddha
a dwelling at each intersection. Each altar

made from whatever stones, sticks, dreams, are at hand,
is a facet of one altar; by noon
the whole city in all its corruption,

all its shed blood the monsoon cannot wash away,
has become a temple,
fragile, insolent, absolute.

i

Of lead and emerald
the reliquary
that knocks my breastbone,

slung round my neck
on a rough invisible rope
that rubs the knob of my spine.

Though I forget you
a red coal from your fire
burns in that box.

ii

On the Times Square sidewalk
we shuffle along, cardboard signs
—Stop the War—
slung round our necks.

The cops
hurry about,
shoulder to shoulder,
comic.

Your high soprano
sings out from just
in back of me—

We shall—I turn,
you're, I very well know,
not there,

238

and your voice, they say,
grew hoarse
from shouting at crowds. . .

yet *overcome*
sounds then hoarsely
from somewhere in front,

the paddywagon
gapes. —It seems
you that is lifted

limp and ardent
off the dark snow
and shoved in, and driven away.

Living

The fire in leaf and grass
so green it seems
each summer the last summer.

The wind blowing, the leaves
shivering in the sun,
each day the last day.

A red salamander
so cold and so
easy to catch, dreamily

moves his delicate feet
and long tail. I hold
my hand open for him to go.

Each minute the last minute.

240

VII   A POEM BY OLGA LEVERTOFF

The Ballad of My Father

'Yáchchiderálum, pútzele mútzele:
  why is your fóotzele burnt to the bone?'
'Hail, dear Rabboni! We would not leave you lonely!
  We come from the limepit where millions were
    thrown!'

My father danced a Hassidic dance the day before he died.
His daughters they were far away, his wife was by his side.

'Yes, from concentration camps, and yes, from gas chambers:
  from thousand years' ghettos, from graves old and new—
Our unremembered bones come to caper in your
    drawingroom,
  and join in the death-dance of one holy Jew!'

He danced for Jesus his Messiah who rose up from the dead
And left the tomb for the upper room and was known
  in the breaking of bread.

'Those who were faithful, and those who betrayed them,
  those who did nothing, and those who defied—
Here they come crowding—the grave has but delayed them:
  your people surround you, in shame and in pride.'

Except you become as a little child my kingdom
  you shall not see.
So he danced in his joy as he did when a boy
  and as often he danced for me.

'Yáchchiderálum, pútzele mútzele:
  faster and faster the measure we tread!
Your hand in my hand, your foot to my footzele—
  partners for ever, the living and the dead!'

243

He danced for those he left long ago and for those
            he never knew,
For an end of strife for eternal life for behold
            I make all things new.

'Come, tread the winepress! The blood of the ages
            squeezed from our flesh shall be our loving cup:
Red river of life, drawn from martyrs and sages,
            shall bear you on its tide till your Lord
                    shall raise you up!'

My father danced a Hassidic dance and sang
            with his latest breath
The dance of peace it will never cease till life
            has conquered death.

'Yáchchiderálum, pútzele mútzele—
            who will remember and who will forget?'
Twirling down time's corridors I see your shadow dancing—
            your song echoes clear down the years whose
                    sun has set.

My father danced and then he died and his name
            is a long time gone.
His voice was stilled and his task fulfilled for a people
            that shall be born.

Yáchchiderálum, pútzele mútzele—
            now if I couldzele I'd speak to you true:
But your dance it is ended and all the tears expended—
            so sleep on and take your rest, my father, my Jew.

                              Olga Levertoff

November, 1963

244

INDEX OF TITLES